Growing Older and Wiser

---

*Coping with Expectations,
Challenges, and Change
in the Later Years*

Nathan Billig, M.D.

LEXINGTON BOOKS
An Imprint of Macmillan, Inc.
New York

Maxwell Macmillan Canada
Toronto

Maxwell Macmillan International
New York   Oxford   Singapore   Sydney

Library of Congress Cataloging-in-Publication Data

Billig, Nathan.
  Growing older and wiser : coping with expectations, challenges, and change in the later years / Nathan Billig.
      p.   cm.
  Includes bibliographical references and index.
  ISBN 0-669-27678-2
  1. Aged—Mental health. 2. Aging—Psychological aspects. 3. Life change events in old age. I. Title.
  RC451.4.A5B5   1992
  613'.043—dc20   92-24310
                                                                                  CIP

Lexington Books
An Imprint of Macmillan, Inc.
866 Third Avenue, New York, N.Y. 10022

Maxwell Macmillan Canada, Inc.
1200 Eglinton Avenue East
Suite 200
Don Mills, Ontario M3C 3N1

Macmillan, Inc. is part of the Maxwell Communication
Group of Companies.

Printed in the United States of America

printing number
1   2   3   4   5   6   7   8   9   10

For
my wife, Gail,
and
my children
Erica, Peter, Andrew, and Deborah

Contents

11 In Conclusion: Being Older and Wiser *219*

Foreword

Americans who have reached age 65 can now expect to live well into their 80s, many beyond. Partly as a result of dramatic advances in medicine and public health and partly as a result of demographic shifts, more and more of us will fall into this category in the next few decades. People over 65 constituted 4 percent of the U.S. population in 1900. By the year 2000, this number will have climbed to over 13 percent. By the year 2025 a fifth of all Americans will be over age 65.

Medical breakthroughs not only have extended life expectancy, they also have helped increase our years of healthy life. We now realize that frailty and mental decline are not the inevitable companions of old age. We know that the processes of "normal" aging can be differentiated from disease processes; that it is possible to prevent and/or treat many of the diseases once thought to be an unavoidable part of aging; and that it is possible to influence the aging process, i.e., to maintain health and quality of life as we age.

As the old stereotypes of aging give way to this new perspective, we each face an array of challenges and opportunities unknown to our grandparents. We must make decisions about health, lifestyle, work, and leisure, decisions that can make a significant difference in our lives for years to come. *Growing Older and Wiser* provides the kind of information we need to make these decisions, cope with the challenges of aging, and plan for our later years to maximize not only the length but also the quality of our lives.

Gene D. Cohen, M.D., Ph.D.
Acting Director
National Institute on Aging

If we really want to live, we'd better start at once to try;
If we don't it doesn't matter, but we'd better start to die.
—W. H. Auden

Preface

There are three ways to approach one's aging: bemoan its arrival and pay a great deal of attention to every change that aging brings; accept the notion passively that getting older is better than the alternative and do the best one can; and try actively to overcome the facts that the body is deteriorating and the mind is not as fast as it used to be and try to do as many of the things one wants to do. People usually draw from one or more of these possibilities at various times and in varying amounts. The people I know who age most happily draw most frequently from the last choice while occasionally and inevitably lapsing into the first two. They know that aging brings many negatives that they wish were not happening. They understand that they are lucky to have relatively full possession of bodily and mental functions. They try to persevere and use all their coping skills even in adversity. They know that time is probably short, and they have an enthusiasm that helps them get as much out of their years as possible, despite the deterioration that is evident.

This book is about understanding some aspects of aging and about coping better in the later years. It is about removing stereotypes and seeing older people for their diversity, strengths, and weaknesses. It is also about facing up to the some of the problems inherent in growing older. The concept of *lifelines*, which I introduce, helps us value the assets of relationships, experiences, and personal qualities that we accumulate over a lifetime. The discussions of depression and dementia point to the need to differentiate aspects of normal aging from disorders that impair functioning in later life and to do as much as possible to limit their impact on successful aging. Depression, one of the most common medical illnesses, is also one of the most treatable.

We are just beginning to understand some aspects of dementia. Until we know more about the causes of and possible treatments for these disorders, we cannot be lax in our care for those whose lives are touched by this catastrophic problem.

This book is about growing older and wiser. Although the two do not necessarily always go together, if we remember and value our lifelines of relationships, experiences, and inherent capabilities, if we learn to cope better and even enjoy our later years, in spite of the deteriorative aspects that may lie ahead, we may be able to both grow older and be wiser.

This book grows out of my interests in aging and in the mental health of older people. I am indebted to the many patients and friends who have taught me about the struggles toward successful aging. They have made it easier for me to write this book and easier to deal with my own aging. I am particularly indebted to three people who nurtured my career as a psychiatrist: Drs. John R. Ross, Jr., Milton Rosenbaum, and Marvin Adland. I thank Dr. Gene D. Cohen for his continuing encouragement of my interests in geriatric psychiatry over the past decade. In addition, I am grateful to my colleagues at Georgetown University and in the Washington, D.C., community for their collegiality and support. Dr. James Foy reviewed parts of the manuscript and offered critical comments, which I value.

Anne Edelstein, my literary agent, and Margaret Zusky, my editor at Lexington Books, have been faithful advocates and advisers in this work.

My wife, Gail Weinmann, has been a loving and patient critic and editor. Her wise advice and support are indispensable.

The Process
of Growing Older

1

Lifelines

99 toll the bells
With a total awareness of time fleeting,
Seasons changing,
Friends gone,
How to adjust?
—G.T., *March 1991*

Few people over the age of 25 look forward to the prospect of aging. Twenty-year-olds dread the notion of the "big 3-0," and people in their 30s think that 40 is surely the beginning of middle age. "Fifty," said one active, healthy, tennis-playing man, only half in jest, "is the beginning of old age, and 65 has been certified as the beginning of the end. After 65, it's just a matter of how long you can hold on, still remember your address and telephone number, and maintain bladder control." The idea that many 75-year-olds maintain careers, businesses, and multiple avocations is foreign to many, and the realization that people 85 years old and older are in the fastest-growing segment of the population is surprising to most.

Aging surely implies deterioration and loss in many respects, but it is a mistake to give up on body and mind easily and before we absolutely must. In a session with students in which a 75-year-old woman was interviewed to demonstrate some of the issues she faced in aging, one student said he had heard that most people over the age of 50 lost their interest in sex. He asked how interested she was at 75? The woman replied rapidly that she thought about sex almost daily; the difficulty at age 75, she found, was finding a like-interested man! She acknowledged that arthritis limited some other activities that she had enjoyed during most of her life, such as tennis and skiing, but she spent very rewarding time in her work as an artist and in various community organizations.

Age is limiting in all kinds of ways and broadening in some others. Genetic predispositions and other biological factors, general state of health, financial resources, life experiences and relationships, coping skills, and personal attitudes greatly affect how limiting and how broadening the process of aging will be. Some of these factors we can do little to alter; others are highly influenced by thoughts, feelings, and actions that are possible to change.

When does aging begin, and when do we feel its impact? These complex questions are now the subject of intensive research. Aging is obviously an ongoing process from the earliest stages of development; we are always "growing older." At some point—and it is a different time for each individual—the deteriorative effects of aging become more extensive and may outweigh the factors that promote growth. Even then, the individual as a whole may be highly functional in most respects. How and when each person feels the impact of these changes depends on a complex mix of biological, psychological, and personality factors. The age of 65 years is merely a historical census marker of the beginning of old age, and recent data disprove its usefulness as a significant milestone in biological, physiological, and psychological terms. Nothing dramatic occurs to most people at or near age 65 and, as a group, people at 65 are not appreciably different, biologically and psychosocially, from those at 55. It is probably not until the middle to late 70s that significant changes occur.

More important than any specific age is the fact that aging is a process that produces enormous variability within the population. Older people are biologically, psychologically, and socially more diverse than any other population sub-group. They are affected, positively and negatively, by the experiences, relationships, illnesses, diet, exercise, medications, and other factors that impact, over the years, on their constitutional base. It is relatively easy to describe the general physical and developmental characteristics of a typical 1-year-old, a 10-year-old, or even a 20-year-old. One-year-olds have weights and heights within a rather narrow range; are largely preverbal; have either just begun to walk or will do so within the next three months; know who makes up their immediate environment and who are strangers; and in a variety of other ways are fairly similar to each other. Even at ages 10 and 20, there is significant homogeneity among age peers. It is far more difficult, maybe impossible, to describe the physical and psychological state of a typical 75-year-old because there are no typical 75-year-olds. They may be entirely competent, healthy, active, independent, and engaged in life, work, or retirement—or frail, depressed, demented, and moribund people who are mostly or entirely dependent on family, friends, other caregivers, or institutions. The range is large and the distribution within the older population wide. At any one point in later life, elderly people as a group are more varied in capacities, activities, experiences, and general functioning than are people at any younger age.

A young woman compared her two 84-year-old grandmothers. Both were in excellent health; both had four children. Both of the grandmothers were well educated and financially comfortable.

One grandmother slept late, moved slowly, and read the obituary notices every day before breakfast to see who she knew had died. She rarely left the house before noon and planned only one event each day so as not to overdo. She was sure to be back from any errands or appointments for a three o'clock nap. She treated herself "carefully" because this is the way she always had been, and, in addition, now she was "old."

The other grandmother was up early every day and quickly did her exercises. She walked her dog in a nearby park before the traffic was heavy and was at the stores to shop as they were opening. She searched the newspapers for free concerts and interesting lectures that did not conflict with her volunteer work at a local hospital.

The young woman wondered what kind of 84-year-old she would be.

It is difficult to speak about "the elderly" as one group, not only because of the great diversity among people at every point in the older age spectrum but also because the age span is long. Infancy, early childhood, adolescence, young adulthood: each is a period of several years to two decades. Old age, extending from 65 or 75 years of age to 100 or 105 years, is almost half a lifetime. People at the earlier end of the range, from 60 to 70, sometimes referred to as "young old," are generally different as a group from the "old old," those from 75 to 85 years, and even more different from those at the later end, at 85 years or more, the oldest old. Those people who live into their 90s to over 100 have some special characteristics, biologically and psychosocially, that we are just beginning to study and do not yet fully understand.

Most older adults are highly functional in most respects, despite having to cope with some symptoms of chronic illness. But attempts to fit older adults into stereotypes abound, and those stereotypes often conspire to permit us to see aging as an entirely negative process in which aging people (all of us) are or will be enfeebled, hopeless, and helpless, or at least tending in that direction. Pejorative terms about being old, frail, and senile are commonly associated with people who are over 65 or 75 years, and, without cause, they are frequently treated as children and as though they are deaf, mentally disturbed, or demented. The vast majority of older adults actually have none of these characteristics. Two vignettes are pertinent.

Dr. J., a prominent 79-year-old physician, was waiting to be fitted with glasses in an optician's office. She was talking in a quiet but animated manner to another customer when she heard the clerk in a booming voice, carefully enunciating every syllable, announce, "Mrs. J., you're next." Dr. J. smiled as she got up from her seat and said to the woman next to her, "He thinks I'm old and deaf, when all I am is a little farsighted."

A 77-year-old attorney and Shakespeare scholar attended a party at which he was the oldest guest by at least ten years, with the majority of the guests having an average age of 45 years. He listened to several conversations around him and offered some opinions about controversial issues in the recent news. The other guests largely did not engage him and treated him as if he were impaired. At one point a guest standing next to the 77-year-old man turned to another to ask what the gentleman's work had been rather than ask the man directly and without realizing that the man might still be working.

There is a danger that people at some arbitrary time will declare themselves "old." If their point is to be more aware to take better care of themselves, to ensure proper nutrition, to exercise regularly, to take medications properly, and to keep up with interests, activities, and relationships because aging may involve some added vulnerabilities, then it is all for the good. Unfortunately, most people who declare themselves "old" are marking the end of an era, the time in which they had been vital. This declaration that life is over or is, at least, drastically changed is dangerous because of the pessimism inherent in it. It affects the way in which we view ourselves, the expectations we have of life, our relationships, activities, interests, and plans. It negatively affects our self esteem. We might not take as good care of ourselves in various ways and might develop a sense of resignation and even doom. There is no point at which we are suddenly "old"; for better and for worse, we are constantly getting older—and possibly wiser. If we declare ourselves "old," we may not have the advantages of either.

"You don't just fall off a cliff at age 65," a 78-year old woman noted. "Life goes on; there are difficult times to be managed and happier times that should be savored." Aging is, in fact, a dynamic developmental phase in the life cycle. People, relationships, ideas, environments continue to change, for better and for worse. It would be incorrect to deny the limitations, disability, losses, and illness inherent in later life for most people. The hair is grayer, and there is less of it; joints are stiffer and more painful with arthritis; people react more slowly; they suffer more and deeper losses than ever before; they feel and are more vulnerable to incapacitating and potentially fatal illnesses. Life seems to, and does in fact, have more uncertainties than ever before. In spite of these negatives, most older people persevere, draw on their strengths, and continue to live and function in their homes and communities. Seventy-five percent of people over 65 years and more than half of those over 85 suffer from neither depression nor dementia, and they enjoy work, retirement, avocations, families, friends, and other aspects of life, dealing successfully with the fact that they are no longer 30, 40, or 50 years old. Among other factors, it is crucial to acknowledge the importance of psychological issues, coping styles and skills, and personality characteristics as considerations in how older adults constructively use or deal with the half of a lifetime that is their later years.

Valuing Lifelines

With aging come inevitable vulnerabilities and specific deterioration of certain systems and functions. Aging also brings with it valuable assets as a result of relationships, experiences, and an appreciation of one's inherent capabilities. These strengths are *lifelines*: the positive forces that can help people to age successfully, to cope better, and to enjoy themselves despite the deteriorative aspects of later life.

Brief or enduring *relationships* of the past and those that begin in or continue into late life are crucial supports, challenging comradeships and great loves that are part, in memories or in reality, of getting older. A 68-year-old man tears up when he talks about still missing a friend who died in fighting in World War II, with whom he shared so many moments of his early life. A 74-year-old woman recalls her first lover and husband with special tenderness and notes how different, and yet how supported, she feels with her second husband. An 82-year-old woman now living in a nursing home recalls that a high school teacher was one of the most important people in her life; because of that relationship, she pursued a career in nursing that lasted almost fifty years. A depressed 70-year-old man admits, with a mixture of pride and shame, that his dog, Rosie, is the most important creature in his life. A 71-year-old man feels proud of his son with whom he has a special bond and a unique friendship. A 69-year-old man values his business partner and close friend with whom he shared all his adult years. For most people, relationships with significant others (including pets) of the past and present enrich life in ways that might not be fully appreciated, even by those who have experienced them. Some of these relationships can start only in younger days; others can be developed and nurtured later in ways that were not possible before. They are a valuable part of our individual histories, and they become a resource, both in memory and in reality, on which to draw in late life.

The older person has had *experiences* that are too numerous to count. Most are mundane and trivial, but some are memorable and a few are unforgettable, even into very late life. They are often linked to special relationships. They form a second aspect of lifelines and represent a part of the self that can be called upon throughout life, and especially in the later years. A 93-year-old grandmother remembers and tells, with girlish excitement, about when the Emperor Franz Josef came to her small town in Austria-Hungary, eighty-five years ago. Everyone cleaned the outside of their houses and dressed up in best clothes for the special occasion. A 78-year-old retired construction foreman points with pride to the houses he built and seems to remember every nail he saw hammered, and a 72-year-old woman thinks that she is so stable and optimistic because, from the time of her early teens, she had to help support her family by working after school. That responsibility, she recalls, made her feel "very important and independent." It sent her off, she thought, for a lifetime of feeling productive and useful. The births, deaths, marriages, anniversaries; happy, sad, and ordinary experiences of daily living; and the special times form a part of the bank of experience that we draw on throughout life. Family rituals, such as regular Friday night or Sunday dinners, and the celebrations of important birthdays and holidays are part of a family history experience that enriches and strengthens everyone. Religious experiences and traditions, for those who have them, and an inner sense of spirituality provide a feeling of a great fellowship and support in difficult times. Experiences of various kinds have a sustaining value and are a reminder of having coped with hard times and enjoyed the good ones. We can continue to do so if we properly value the experiences of our lifetime and attempt to use them to influence the present and future.

In addition to personal life experiences, people are enriched by the world and local events through which they live. They become part of the individual experience and also a generally shared history. Living through the Great Depression, World's Fairs, the Sunday morning on which Pearl Harbor was bombed, the first landing on the moon, the days on which Franklin Roosevelt, John F. Kennedy, and Martin Luther King, Jr., died remind us of eras of history, times of our lives through which we struggled, coped, or celebrated. These events became parts of the people who experienced the contemporary pain and/or drama of those events and offer perspectives of self and others quite different from those who read about them in books or even study them intensely.

Long-standing *individual personality characteristics* change very little with normal aging.* Old people are not bitter any more than young people are irresponsible. People seem to age with many of the lifelong personality characteristics they possessed earlier, although times of great stress might temporarily affect their expression. The retired construction foreman no longer lifts 100-pound timbers or risks climbing up thirty-foot ladders, but his take-charge manner and his dependability are evident in many ways at 78, and he still can teach his grandson how to build a "proper garage" and re-roof the house "better than anyone else." An 89-year-old woman provides a steadying influence, as she always has, when her adult children face illness and crises in their lives. She had owned a men's clothing shop in the days when few women owned and operated businesses. She still knows the line-up of the New York Yankees and checks the box scores daily. The aggressive, stubborn 77-year-old man is

*Robert R. McCrae and Paul T. Costa, Jr., *Personality in Adulthood* (New York: Guilford Press, 1990).

tolerated by his children and grandchildren, although he regularly tries their patience; he is only slightly more demanding than he has always been, but he has endured recent losses and significant illness. His aggressiveness has allowed him to overcome personal challenges, such as survival through the ravages of Europe during World War II. A 90-year-old woman, though quite frail, takes time almost every day to draw or paint, something from which she has derived much satisfaction for over sixty years. Her artwork has changed considerably over those years. She says, "It's now more mature than it used to be and maybe a bit more somber, like I am." Her creativity is a valuable gift that she does not want to lose; "it's a part of me." Inherent capabilities and personality qualities are the most often forgotten or denied aspects of the lifelines of older people, and yet they are the most durable. They are part of the core of our being and are not subject to the diminished memory of which so many complain. They are assets to be highly valued because they can be called up repeatedly while facing the variable circumstances of aging.

Among the most crucial personality characteristics at any age, but in the later years, in particular, is the capacity for *hope* and *optimism*. It greatly colors one's view of life and is a powerful asset in surviving stresses, traumas, and tragedies of life, from adolescence through later life. Hope implies believing that one has the will and the means to accomplish tasks and goals, despite obstacles. People who are pessimistic and have little hope are more vulnerable to being overwhelmed by even the relatively minor and inevitable stresses of daily life, from medical illness to leaky roofs and broken-down cars. In the later years, the small stresses can add up, until they seem exaggerated, unmanageable, or even devastating. Sometimes people can be reminded of their inherent capacity for hope and optimism, which had been evident earlier in their lives. For those in whom there is little evidence of past hopefulness, counseling can be helpful to assess current stresses more realistically and to see future situations with a more optimistic, or at least less pessimistic, view. Having a more hopeful outlook generally serves one not only in the immediate situation but as a model for later and possibly more significant stresses.

> Ms. D. is a 73-year-old woman who worked for many years as a housekeeper. She lived alone in an old house, worked part-time, and had various community activities. After helping with a large project at her church just before Thanksgiving, she was fatigued and somewhat sad. She felt that she did not have the energy to "face the holidays," although in the past she had typically enjoyed them with family and friends. During that week, she had lost a filling in a tooth, noticed a leak in the roof of the house, and had to replace the water heater. The dentist thought she needed more extensive dental work performed than she had anticipated, and the roof needed several large patches. She felt that she did not have the ability to get through the "snowball of stresses," although she admitted that at a younger age she had felt robust; she had regularly handled much more. A friend pointed out that she had always been an optimistic person who believed she could get through almost anything. Ms. D. assumed that the combination of events allowed her to exaggerate the view that she and her world were falling apart and to "forget" her capacity for hopefulness and her strengths to get through some difficult weeks.

Too often older adults who are faced with multiple losses, medical illness, disability, and everyday stresses that everyone encounters fail to focus on and use these lifelines—the vast personal assets of relationships, experiences, and inherent capabilities they have established over the years. In contrast to the deterioration of aging, the lifelines are the other side of the ledger: the positive forces that can and must be drawn on in the aging process. They are proof of strengths older adults have possessed and probably still do; they are evidence of the ability to cope and enjoy and must not be forgotten or denied; they are resources and supports, in fact and in spirit, to muster and maintain. They are lifelines to successful aging.

Integrity versus Despair

The concept of lifelines derives heavily from the thoughtful and eloquent work of Erik Erikson. In what has become one of the most respected descriptions of human development, Erikson outlined eight psychosocial stages of the life cycle, from infancy through old age, through which people pass in the process of development. Erikson defined a struggle between opposing forces that occurs at each stage of development in the life cycle. Out of these struggles emerge certain personal strengths that are crucial to continued optimal development.* (Erikson's psychosocial stages of life are shown in Figure 1–1, somewhat changed in terminology from the original work.) In infancy there is the struggle of *basic trust versus basic mistrust,* out of which emerges *hope.* In later childhood, there is the conflict between *industry* and *inferiority,* from which evolves *competence;* in adolescence, *identity versus identity diffusion* produces *fidelity.* In adulthood, *care* emerges from the struggle between *generativity* and *stagnation;* and in old age *integrity versus despair* produces *wisdom.* At each stage, the individual has the opportunity to achieve the strengths obtainable at that time and also to rework early phases. At each stage, the person may reexperience the tensions that were inadequately integrated earlier. To a great extent, successful developmental progress depends on building on the strengths that emerge at each of the earlier times.

Focusing on the later years, Erikson uses the concept of *integrity* to mean a coming to terms with one's life, accepting oneself and one's strengths and weaknesses, and integrating one's life experiences, relationships, and circumstances, even in the face of the often distressing aspects of decline of the later years. To accomplish the integration required in this last stage, the individual must be amenable to remembering and reviewing earlier experiences. Successful mastery of this phase of life, in Erikson's terms, produces wisdom, a quality that enhances the later years and allows one to be *vitally involved* with life. Erikson, now

*Erik H. Erikson, *Childhood and Society* (New York: Norton, 1963).

FIGURE 1–1
Psychosocial Stages of Life

	1	2	3	4	5	6	7	8
Old age								Integrity versus despair WISDOM
Adulthood							Generativity versus self-absorption CARE	
Young adulthood						Intimacy versus isolation LOVE		
Adolescence					Identity versus confusion FIDELITY			
School age				Industry versus inferiority COMPETENCE				
Play age			Initiative versus guilt PURPOSE					
Early childhood		Autonomy versus shame, doubt WILL						
Infancy	Basic trust versus basic mistrust HOPE							

Source: E. H. Erikson, J. M. Erikson, and H. Q. Kivnick, *Vital Involvement in Old Age* (New York: Norton, 1986).

more than 90 years old himself, is clearly optimistic about the capacity of each of us to be vitally involved in later life. He has continued to revise his ideas and to write and speak about them. Erikson's scheme for the life cycle, including old age, is a dynamic one in which each stage is dependent on earlier ones and builds for the future. Each stage has individual characteristics essential to the whole. The later years are a vital part of the process.

Life Review

Dr. Robert Butler, the first director of the National Institute on Aging and a noted American psychiatrist, developed the idea of *life review* in the early 1960s.* This concept complements Erikson's work and refers to the inevitable review of life's experiences and relationships that people go through as they age. Older adults not only review and assess the past but also attempt to think about what they can do with the rest of their lives and what they may leave to the next generation. Review and reminiscence, informally with friends or family members or through psychotherapy, can help clarify unresolved issues. For some people, themes of loss and vulnerability are overwhelming; these individuals may need some help in mourning relationships and experiences of the past, even the rather distant past. Reminiscence allows one to look at situations and relationships of the past and to reflect on coping skills used at difficult times and on the capacities to enjoy the pleasures of earlier years. These skills and capacities can be retrieved and renovated, if needed and not immediately available, to be used again in later life. Life review can renew a sense of mastery, and if it is communicated to others, it may reinforce a sense of pride of transmitting a personal history to someone else.

A 79-year-old woman sought counseling to deal with her life-long distress about her older sister, whom she described as a

*Robert N. Butler, "The Life Review," *Psychiatry* 26 (1963): 65–76.

bitter, envious woman who had never been a friend to her. When the 83-year-old sister broke her hip and had other medical complications, the younger sister thought that this was an opportunity to be of real help and perhaps to get the recognition for which she had yearned for more than 75 years. Her offers were rejected, and the sister died several months later. Counseling, using life review techniques, helped the younger woman mourn the loss not only of her 83-year-old sister but of the sister she wished for but had never had. For the first time, the woman realized how much thought and energy she had devoted to the distress concerning her sister. She felt that a lifelong ache had been alleviated, and now she had more energy for other people and activities.

As people live longer, life review may be done regularly, periodically, or over some years, dealing with some issues at one time and others at later. Reminiscence has clear benefits for those who do it and also serves the listeners, who may discover facts and feelings even about a person they thought they had known well. Reminiscence can help build relationships with people across generations who may, in fact, have achieved and also may impart some of the wisdom Erikson values so highly.

As we do a life review and struggle to integrate our lives rather than face despair, as we draw on our lifelines of relationships, experiences, and inherent capabilities and personality, we open up the possibility of seeing the later years not as the beginning of the end but as part of a dynamic continuum, with its certain crises, disabilities, vulnerabilities, and trials but also opportunities and joys. Some of the former can be lessened or mastered, and some of the latter can certainly be maximized.

2

Relationships with Children and Grandchildren

"**T**hey have their own lives; I don't want to be a burden to them." How many times have we heard (or said) that? If we have done our jobs well as parents, our children and grandchildren do have their own lives. Optimally, we all have our own lives, pursuing significant relationships, working, playing, and coping with the struggles that life inevitably brings. But even for rather independent people, friends and family are valuable resources to share the good times and for help with the difficult ones.

Our society has changed dramatically since today's older adults were young adults. The extended family is more fragmented, geographically and otherwise, and only rarely do several generations live under one roof. More women seek professional careers and other employment opportunities, and they are less available for volunteer work and family support. Older people are living longer, and there are more of them. Most older people are independent and manage their lives much as they did when they were younger. But as we age, we may want to spend more time with children and grandchildren, to get gratification from watching them grow and mature, to assist them to cope better with their lives and to relieve difficulties that often come with aging.* It is entirely normal to hear the ticking clock, even faintly, and perhaps to be frightened by that, to want or need more support or to feel quite urgently, "I have to get it all in

*Although I mention only children and grandchildren, I also include other members of the younger generations with whom older adults, particularly those without children, interact—nephews, nieces, and young friends.

before I die." Family members serve a crucial function when they can appreciate or accommodate the normal, healthy desires and needs of older adults to relate over several generations. Parents and grandparents similarly have an invaluable role in providing support and bringing a sense of continuity to the family system. Sometimes conflicts between parents and children that arose many years before are still alive or are dormant just below the surface; they are difficult to resolve. Across the generations there is a need to value the emotional and historical assets of family, tolerate the idiosyncrasies and petty annoyances, heal the old wounds, and work out the conflicts, when possible.

Changing Roles and Responsibilities

The interactions of aging parents, even healthy ones, and adult children, even the most devoted ones, can often be characterized by significant tensions on both sides. When relatives have medical illness, psychiatric problems, marital stresses, or other difficulties, the ability to be flexible and to tolerate possibly changing roles is significantly challenged and put at risk. Some older adults are acutely stressed or chronically ill and need intermittent or regular, even daily, help, for varying amounts of time, from family members, friends, or other caregivers. These conditions create strains in relationships within the nuclear family that need to be acknowledged and dealt with.

> Mr. and Mrs. J. sought consultation for themselves and Mrs. J.'s recently widowed 80-year-old mother, Mrs. T., who moved into their home from another city. Mrs. T. had not coped well in her own apartment since the death of her husband six months earlier and could think of nothing better than moving into her daughter's house. Mr. J. was a reasonably accepting and empathic man who liked his mother-in-law but resented her wish to monopolize her daughter's attention in the evenings, after the Mr. and Mrs. J.'s returned from work, to question them about their dinners out with friends, to talk incessantly about her deceased husband of

fifty-five years, and to complain frequently about the recent recurrence of arthritis, which was not disabling. Mr. and Mrs. J. were also concerned that Mrs. T. was essentially alone all day in their suburban house with little inclination or opportunity to socialize with other people. Their two adult children lived in the metropolitan area and saw their grandmother approximately monthly.

The consultation and some consequent visits provided opportunities for all to vent their feelings and for some goals and plans to be made to structure schedules and relationships within the household, and to help Mrs. T. participate in activities in the community that might be stimulating and enjoyable for her. Mrs. J. obtained information about social and educational programs that might be appropriate for her mother. In three to six months, they would reconsider the living arrangement. At three months, Mrs. T. had several new friends, was regularly attending an educational and arts program at a nearby community center, was cooking and baking at home, and was accepting of the fact that the Mr. and Mrs. J. had busy professional and social lives. Although she would have liked more social time with them, Mrs. T. preferred their uncertain daily involvement with her to living elsewhere, and all felt content with the current arrangement. The fact that Mrs. T. was relatively healthy and was cognitively intact made it possible for her to be independent. If any of these factors changed, the situation might have had to be significantly modified and other supports initiated.

In some instances family members must deal with their helplessness, anger, and subsequent guilt concerning their older relatives for whom the options are not so bright.

A 51-year-old single woman with an active career was called by her father's neighbor, in another city, to say that her father was spending a considerable amount of time roaming around the neighborhood in the evenings in what appeared to be a somewhat disoriented state. He seemed to make it home each night, and in telephone conversations with his daughter he said everything was "fine." She made a trip to visit him and found that he and his apartment were disheveled, his refrigerator contained no edible food, and unpaid bills and other mail had accumulated over several months. He talked about all the good things he had been doing, but he was vague and had almost no short-term memory. She brought him home with her and made appointments for evaluation of his physical and mental state. Medical examinations revealed that he was malnourished and probably had some form of progressive dementia. The daughter could not care for him in her small apartment, and together they had insufficient assets for him to live in an apartment with assistance. She decided that he should enter a nursing home, at least temporarily, so that he could be stabilized, nourished, and more fully evaluated. The older man was devastated to be taken, in a matter of weeks, from his familiar environment in another city and was upset that he could not at least live with his daughter. His daughter felt she had failed to keep in adequate contact with him during the past year, had wanted to see him as doing well when he was not, and now was incapable of taking care of him.

"Our parents are not supposed to have difficulties when they do, just when we are trying to deal with our own marriages, children, careers, and mortality," say their adult children. "They were supposed to take care of us!" For many adult children, seeing parents grow older and needing assistance of various kinds is painful because of the stark awareness that they are losing their real or idealized caretaking parents or the ones they never had. They are pushed to give up any remaining childlike hopes of dependency and assume the roles of the next older generation. Adult children may feel sad to see their parents, who were vital and strong earlier in their lives, have pain, illness, or even reasonable limitations that they never associated with them. On a practical level, the time, effort, and frustration inherent in assisting them with their infirmities is often extensive. It is difficult to change long-established family roles, but that is just another part of growing up and older, even if it occurs after we think we are grown up. One measure of maturity or good mental health is the flexibility, sometimes painful, to modify roles as changes in circumstances and relationships dictate. Growing older and watching others who are close to us grow older challenges us to be flexible, to revise our expectations, and to make the most of our capabilities.

Daughters and daughters-in-law, when they exist, bear the primary responsibility for assisting their older parents when they need help.* Ellen Goodman, a Boston writer, has said that the guilt about being a working daughter has replaced the guilt about being a working mother.† Some mental health professionals believe that the mother-daughter relationship is the most vulnerable to tension and conflict, even under the best circumstances. The added stress of an illness or a period of dependency in a parent requires special efforts by both the parent (often the mother) and the daughter. Unresolved issues between adult children and parents, dating back many years, often have to be faced so that the crisis at hand can be mastered. An 81-year-old man had never gotten over the insult that his son refused to go into the family business; that upset tainted their relationship for twenty-five years. An older woman was still angry at age 83 that her daughter had, thirty-seven years earlier, "left her alone as a widow" to get her own apartment, "and she wasn't even getting married." The incidents may sound trivial, but in the minds of the parents and children, they had great real and symbolic meaning and resulted in deep wounds, which were not effectively resolved. Adult children can learn from these experiences and *try to do it differently* with their children. They may go through this again as they age and ask for support from the next generation. To a great extent, the manner in which grandparents are treated serves as a model for the treatment of parents by *their* children. Children are watching and learning as their parents show their capacity for care and concern for their own older parents.

*Elaine M. Brody, *Women in the Middle: Their Parent-Care Years* (New York: Springer Publishing Co., 1990).
†Ellen Goodman, "Pediatrics to Geriatrics," *Boston Globe*, May 21, 1985.

Parents also have to adjust to new roles, recognizing that their children are now adults; that they have new obligations, loyalties, and responsibilities; that they are capable of making decisions for themselves and their children, but they may forever want to get some advice or support at difficult times or even regularly. It is a difficult line to tread: to have a life of one's own, to be involved, interested, and supportive of the lives of children but being careful not intrude on their autonomy. Older parents have to work out the extent to which they should visit their adult children, call on the telephone, comment on or criticize their behavior, and monitor their schedules. Older parents may have to learn to say "no" to some of the ongoing requests of their children. It may be difficult to keep giving them money or to be as available as one's children would like, for babysitting. One 77-year-old woman felt that she always was on call to babysit for her grandchildren so that her daughter could play tennis: "Mostly I don't mind, but sometimes it interferes with my meetings or activities and I have trouble saying no." Adult children can help their parents by thinking about the limits to which they can and should intrude on their parents' lives. Some do not see their parents as having interests, responsibilities, and activities separate from their children that at times may clash with the children's needs.

Parents must also adjust their expectations of what their children can and want to do for them. Although they are adults, children do not want to hear much about parents' aches and pains, marital problems, or other stresses in their lives. Children think that parents should take care of themselves, just as parents expect adult children to take care of themselves. Children do not automatically have an obligation to parent their parents. But filial devotion is not dead, and most children do come to the aid of their parents in distress. At some point, parents decided to have the responsibility of parenthood, and they are always parent to the child, although that relationship changes in character over the years and at particular times during the years. Each parent and adult child pair works out a balance between involvement, interest, and support on the one hand and mutual respect for autonomy on the other. The nature of individual family relationships over the years is a powerful influence on the extent to which this can be accomplished.

> One 55-year-old man described, with a good-natured smile, a scene in which he and his family left his widowed mother's house after a weekend visit. He and his wife helped their own four children into the car for the three-hour ride home. As he said a final good-bye to his mother, the 78-year-old woman asked her grown son, "Did *you* remember to go to the bathroom?"

Older adults, particularly independent ones, may have trouble with the notion that they may need to depend on their children, for a brief time or extended periods. For many older people, the idea of dependency is humiliating and guilt provoking; for others, it brings the prospect of welcome assistance.

> One older man expressed great pride that his busy son took the time to visit potential assisted-living residences with him. He had never wanted to lean on his children and always thought of his son, who now had a family of his own, as dependent on *him*. It was a relief to the 75-year-old father that he finally did not have to take care of his children. If necessary, they would be available to take care of him. That was reassuring even to this independent man.

After years of being and feeling independent, needing one's children's support, even in the short term, to manage aspects of one's life can be difficult. Sensitivity of adult children to the threats to parental autonomy and embarrassment, sometimes alternating with parental relief, is required. Children must also be careful that they become aware of their own limits to involve themselves in their parents' lives. Wearing oneself out in an effort to give care will result in a cascade of anger, guilt, sadness, and fatigue. At times, and in certain circumstances, the ability to seek assistance from social agencies, physicians, and others is a valuable skill that can be developed.

Envy and Its Consequences

Particularly through the later years, people may be envious of the younger generations who are healthy and vigorous and seem to have so many options. A 55-year-old man bemoans the fact that he is no longer a match for his 18-year-old son on the tennis court. While that is to be regretted, he ignores the fact that his son wants to spend time with him, playing tennis. If he could accept his son's prowess graciously and admiringly, he could savor the other aspects of their relating on the tennis court.

> Mr. H., a 74-year-old man, has trouble accepting his 32-year-old son-in-law's casual attitude toward life. He never wears a tie and jacket to work, seems unconcerned with saving money for the future, and whenever he is taken to dinner orders one of the most expensive items on the menu. He admits that the young man is bright and ambitious, has a good job, and is a caring husband and father, but those other attributes irritate the older man. He knows that these feelings are not right but cannot overlook them.

In fact, Mr. H. was envious of his son-in-law's freedom. The young man was vigorous, energetic, involved with the development of his children, and married to an attractive young woman, Mr. H.'s daughter. As a young man, Mr. H. had worked two jobs to support his family and pay his tuition to school during the depression years of the 1930s; he never took a vacation, went out to restaurants, or had much fun during his 30s. He worked hard and had little patience for people who were so relaxed about life. A friend advised him to spend more time with his son-in-law to try to get to know some of the admirable aspects of his personality and life-style and also to realize that the way Mr. H. grew up was difficult and not necessarily the only way to do it, given other circumstances.

> A 69-year-old mother of two daughters is doting and attentive to them and their families, but it is apparent to the daughters that their mother does not want to hear about their

work experiences. When they attempt to talk to her about their jobs, she says, "Oh, isn't that nice," and changes the subject quickly. The daughters knew that their mother had wished to go to college and pursue a career, but financial pressures in her family prevented her. She had married a businessman when she was 19 years old, worked briefly as an office clerk, and then stayed home to take care of the children. They recognize her sensitivity to and great envy of their relative successes, and they refrain from challenging her. Talking about work is not a necessary part of their relationships with her.

Older adults can recognize their envy of the vigor, success, health, and array of options possessed by their youthful children and grandchildren at the same time that they admire and care for these loved ones. Acknowledging feelings of envy is the first step to mastering it; they need not interfere with precious relationships.

Younger people often greatly admire the status, experiences, wisdom, and other attributes of their older relatives. They may respect the achievements of a parent or grandparents, their ability to have mastered difficult situations, and the ways in which they contributed to the family and the subsequent generations. Younger people find ways to express that admiration and appreciation to their parents and grandparents, to share in those past achievements and family history. Ironically, the older generation may even find themselves the object of envy by the young, who may view their older relatives as being fortunate to have come to terms with their lives while they still struggle to define themselves and sort out options.

Special Relationships

Aside from the difficult issues, there are some significant and often overlooked benefits in the later years for relationships with children and grandchildren. One is the great pleasure that older adults can have in relating to their adult children, nephews, nieces, or younger friends as the mature people they have become. A special relationship that combines friendship with a pride in having been an essential part of the growth of the child is possible. Those who experience this adult child-parent friendship often see it as an unexpected bonus of the middle and later years. Sometimes old disappointments in each other and unrealized hopes and expectations, realistic and unrealistic, can be acknowledged and worked through and/or put aside, so that the later years can be more fulfilling to the older parents and their adult children and relatives. The scars of earlier hurts, however, cannot always easily be dismissed, and the relationships between generations may remain strained. That is a loss that both young and old must mourn.

Grandchildren and grandparents can offer each other unique and relatively conflict-free relationships. Grandparents can serve as an emotional buffer between parents and children; their home can be a haven to which to retreat when conflicts with or pressures of parents are too great. The give and take between the more distant generations often avoids the expectable stresses that can be present between parent and child, at almost any age. Those relationships, even if variable because of intercurrent illness, travel, or personal absorption, should be encouraged for the mutual benefits of time spent together. Children learn much about their family's history and dynamics through grandparents, and grandparents often say that they can spoil their grandchildren in a way they could not their own children. In some families, grandparents assume the major child-rearing responsibilities of their grandchildren, especially when a single parent must work or because a family crisis prevents the parents from taking care of their children. Grandparents, of course, offer grandchildren much more than "spoiling" and feel gratified that they can contribute to raising a new generation of their family. One grandmother said she loved the visits of her grandchildren—the cooking she did, the places she took them, the songs they taught her, and the fact that they went home to their parents when the vacation was over. The availability of active and involved grandparents can offer the parents and children a valuable supportive family network, especially when old conflicts are comfortably resolved.

One young man recounted the years, between ages 8 and 12, when he spent every Saturday afternoon and evening alone with his maternal grandparents. He confessed to being a little concerned about their frailty and wondered, "What if something happens to them." He mostly recalled the rather mundane and ritualistic things he did with them: the walks in the neighborhood when they always stopped at the ice cream store for a dessert or listening to his grandmother's seemingly endless stories about the old country. What came through to him was a special caring that they had for him that he experienced with no one else in quite the same way.

Mrs. M., an 80-year-old piano teacher, found that weekly visits to teach her 6-year-old granddaughter how to play the piano were among the highlights of her week. They played, sang, and talked together, and then she joined the family for dinner. What a storehouse of memories they would both have of that special relationship!

3

Loss, Loneliness, and Bereavement

To everything there is a season, and a time to every
purpose under the heaven.
A time to be born, and a time to die; a time to plant, and
a time to pluck up that which is planted; . . .
A time to weep, and a time to laugh; a time to mourn,
and a time to dance.
—Ecclesiastes 3:1–2,4

Loss, loneliness, and bereavement are three of the most common and most difficult emotional issues with which older people must cope. Older adults are bombarded by loss: the loss of spouses and friends through illness and death, loss of health, esteem, employment, status, homes of many years, acuity of senses, and stamina. It is amazing that anyone deals with these successfully, and yet, most people do cope well. Losses usually are a part but not the predominant part of the later years. Coping with loss brings serious emotional stress at any age, and the extent to which individuals have the capacity to deal with it may be the degree to which they can maintain mental health. With loss comes sadness, grief, and, possibly, loneliness. These are not disorders or symptoms of illness but rather normal reactions to serious life events. They are among what Judith Viorst has aptly labeled the "necessary losses" of life.*

*Judith Viorst, *Necessary Losses* (New York: Simon and Schuster, 1986).

There is clearly a hierarchy of losses in everyone's life, and the extent of grief may vary with the nature and timing of the loss, one's own sense of stability at the time, and one's general way of coping with crisis and catastrophe. The death of a spouse, usually regarded as the most catastrophic loss, particularly after a long and successful marriage, may never be completely grieved; it is entirely normal to be sad and maybe even to cry on every day for the rest of one's life. The deaths of other family members and of close friends can also be devastating losses to an older person. Older adult survivors feel increasingly alone, without the support and camaraderie of a generational network and the friendship supports they have long cherished.

Timetables and stages of grief are difficult to predict because of individual characteristics, but with each succeeding month, there should be some progress toward relating better to important people and activities. Certainly there are religious and societal rituals and standards that mark various mourning activities and stages at one week, one month, or one year, but it is clear that normal mourning has no timetable. It may extend over two, three, or more years, with a gradual recovery and sometimes an incomplete one. People deal best with loss when they experience the sadness, loneliness, and grief for a period of time and do not necessarily try to ignore it. Being "brave" is not particularly useful for the mourner. Women tend to be more open in their mourning; they live longer than men, usually survive their spouses, if they have them, and thus have more experience with grief and mourning. Most men still have difficulty being open about their feelings, particularly about the sad ones; there is often a premium put on "being strong." Yet although they may not mourn in an outwardly apparent way, nevertheless they may experience sadness and emptiness in more subtle ways, such as with lack of concentration at work, irritability attributed to other causes, loss of appetite, and sleeplessness. They may be intolerant of other people who more obviously express these feelings. Generally, those who mourn according to individual schedules, coping mechanisms, personalities, and life-styles stand the best chance of recovery from the life crisis of a catastrophic loss.

Mrs. B., a 72-year-old woman, consulted me about her grief reaction to her 67-year-old sister's death three months earlier. She felt "empty, profoundly sad, and lonely." "I've lost my best friend, she said." She was tearful and experiencing insomnia and decreased interest in her usual activities. She felt guilty that she had not told her sister all the positive things she now thought to tell her, such as how supportive she had been when Mrs. B. had gone through some difficult years. Two years earlier, another younger sister had died. Mrs. B. was now the lone survivor of her family of origin.

Mrs. B. came for the consultation primarily because her physician, her husband, and her children thought she was "overreacting" and "should be over it by now." She was getting up at her usual time in the morning, getting dressed, and, at least, "going through the motions" of her usual activities. She went to lunch with friends occasionally and had just begun attending a class that she had enjoyed prior to her sister's death. In the interview, this well-dressed and -groomed woman was tearful when talking about her sister and the feelings of extreme loss. She spoke about the shock of the death, coming just four months after the diagnosis of cancer was made. She was appropriate in all respects.

Mrs. B. was mourning the loss of her last close relative, a sister whom she dearly loved and who had been of great help to her through the years. The grief reaction was an entirely normal response to the death of her sister, and I told Mrs. B. that she would probably have these feelings for many months to come, gradually resuming her ability to enjoy activities and pleasurable aspects of her life. The scar resulting from the death would always be with her. Mrs. B. was relieved that she was not odd in her reaction and felt reassured that she could stand up to her husband's stoicism about such matters.

"She only wants to talk about my father, and she does that all day long," a young man whose father had died six months earlier, said of his mother. "And she thinks there's something wrong with me because I don't." Three to six months after such a loss, most widows talk a great deal about their deceased spouse. The talking is probably helpful to them, but it can be enormously stressful to relatives and friends who deal with grief in different ways. In addition, children are often intolerant of their parents' disabilities, even when it is acute and results from a reasonable crisis such as the death of a spouse. Some of these children may deal with their loss of a deceased parent differently than the surviving parent may expect them to grieve. This conflict may deprive both of them of the support they need.

In the first three months after a loss, survivors experience sadness, significant sleeplessness, decreased appetite, periods of crying, and loss of interest and enjoyment in most activities. They may take on attributes or habits of the deceased person. They may express guilt over what was done or not done for the deceased in the last months or even years. Surviving spouses and other family members may simultaneously feel a sense of relief that the death had occurred, particularly after a long illness in which the deceased had been in an extended coma, had had great pain, was seriously disabled, or had suffered major personality changes or dementia. In those situations, people say, "It was merciful; he's really better off; he wasn't really living for some time." Even when this is true, the death heralds the end of a life, and perhaps a generation or an era. Survivors reflect on what they experienced with the person and the fact that none of that can occur again or be changed. Talking about memories is a way to mourn and also an attempt to maintain a living memorial.

Sometimes feelings of great loss are mixed up with residual angry feelings toward the deceased that may not be fully conscious. Even if they were, it is certainly not permissible for most people to talk about negative feelings. Anger may have to do with the fact of the death and being left alone, the retirement that never happened, the dreams unrealized, or the relationship that never lived up to expectations. If anger is present and unacknowledged over a period of time, it may fester and become the seed of more serious difficulties.

The immediate weeks of mourning are usually accompanied by attention from family and friends; the weeks and months that follow are a difficult time for bereaved older adults. During that time, survivors need encouragement to engage in activities, invitations to participate with others, and support in their self-care. Missing the companionship of the deceased spouse brings despair, and having to manage daily life alone, perhaps for the first time in adult life, is frightening. The pain of loss, the loneliness, the prospect of facing life without a companion, and the wish to be independent and brave all come in waves over an extended period of mourning. For most people, personal strengths, supportive friends and family, and a life routine help to restore a framework for functioning.

In spite of tragic loss and long-term grief, older adults can enjoy many aspects of life with new and old relationships, activities, and interests. Sometimes they and their children do not appreciate the capacity they have to "go on living" while still remembering and missing a deceased loved one. One recently widowed older man summed it up: "After sixty-two years of marriage, I feel like I had an amputation, but I guess I can learn to walk again, maybe with a bit of a limp." An 80-year-old woman who had not spent a night without her husband in fifty-one years of marriage until he died five years ago confessed that every morning and every evening she still cried, "just for two or three minutes," when she realized he was no longer there.

Sometimes grief does not seem to abate with time; the survivor remains incapacitated or becomes increasingly depressed. Taking to bed during the day, continued insomnia after the first few months, neglecting to eat or otherwise take care of oneself, persistent physical complaints, withdrawal from relationships with significant people, thoughts of worthlessness or hopelessness, and expressions of suicidal thoughts at any time are symptoms that should be taken seriously by family and friends and evaluated by a professional. Although physicians are reluctant to medicate with antidepressants in the early grieving period and may prescribe only a tranquilizer for temporary insomnia, an extended or abnormal bereavement may require psychotherapy and/or medications to assist with recovery.

Grieving may be greatly complicated when the surviving spouse has been particularly dependent on his or her mate or when the relationship, no matter how long, has been marked by significant conflict and anger.

> A 72-year-old retired attorney sought consultation for persistent, chronic depression three years after the death of his wife. Throughout their marriage of more than forty years, he had been primarily involved in his work, and she raised their three children, managed the household, and organized their social life. "I never had to think about a meal, the children's clothing, or what we were doing with friends on the weekend," he said. Two years prior to her death, Mrs. H. had had a stroke and was paralyzed on the right side of her body. One year later, she had a second stroke and was bedridden, and Mr. H. retired to help take care of her. "I did things I had never done in my life; I cooked, cleaned, and ran errands." Daily he sat by his wife's bed for many hours. After his wife's death, Mr. H. became quite helpless and reverted to the dependent state that had characterized most of his marriage. He lived alone in the house he and his wife had occupied, he rarely cleaned, he ate as many meals as possible at a local diner, and mail accumulated, unanswered, in large piles. He did not understand why he had regressed, when during her illness he had "taken care of everything."

In psychotherapy Mr. H. talked about his loneliness since his wife's death and his dependency on her for "the everyday things of life." He had difficulty expressing his feelings, saying that he "wasn't good at that." Although he had met several women "who wanted to take care of him," he was still lonely and found it almost impossible to initiate social arrangements with people. "When someone calls to invite me, I'll go." A daughter lived nearby, but he did not want to bother her; he saw her and her family on weekends and enjoyed that. He had had no significant friendships at the time of his wife's death. When he was involved in activities, he felt better, but at home he was sad. His physician thought that he seemed depressed. After some months of talking and with the help of antidepressant medications, Mr. H. became less sad and began spending more time with several people he had met through various community activities. His basically shy, rather passive personality characteristics remained the same.

Although mourning may go on for some years, there is normally a progression toward more usual activities and life-style. Some people have always denied the sadder parts of their lives and "snap back" easily; others take longer to mourn. Tolerance for a personal style of adapting is essential; there is no right way to do it. Resorting to tranquilizers, over-the-counter medications, alcohol, or frenzies of activities to anesthetize oneself from the mourning experience is dangerous, and possibly lethal.

Mourning is a time to get back to lifelines of relationships, experiences, and inherent capabilities and to use them in healing. It is a time to take stock of friends and acquaintances, even to make list of those people to call regularly on the telephone for support in a lonely moment, to make plans for an activity, or just to chat. Those who are mourning need to think about individual experiences and events that might sustain them, entertain them, help them feel stronger, and that might be repeated in perhaps another way, with different people. And it is a time to value inherent capabilities and personal strengths and weaknesses—the characteristics to muster in dealing with new challenges.

Even in the absence of an immediate or profound loss, many older people are lonely. Some have never been good at making and maintaining friendships, and others find the later years isolating because of chronic illnesses, retirement, relative immobility, and a sense of futility about new ventures in later years. Some see the later years as a time of disengagement from the people and activities of the past—sometimes by choice, sometimes not. Older people tend to spend more time alone than they did in earlier years. Some of that can be "good" time, with solitary activities, time for reflection, taking care of oneself. They value their solitude. Being alone does not necessarily mean being lonely. But there is a danger that a significant retreat from people, activities, and socialization may predispose to depression and poor general health. Many studies demonstrate the beneficial effects of maintaining social and avocational interests through the later years.

Loneliness is a difficult but not insurmountable, problem. Most communities have one or more social or activity centers that help older people join others for common interests, fun, and the possibility of friendship. The loneliness of the later years presents another opportunity and challenge to rekindle and draw on one's lifelines of relationships, experiences, and inherent capabilities. Sometimes older people must be reminded of these assets and supported to look for ways to use them in difficult times. Lifelines not only support and strengthen people internally; they are a framework through which individuals can relate to others, without having had college degrees, particular skills, or even what many consider to have been a very exciting life. Everyone has had deeply personal and more casual relationships with others, experiences that have engaged them, and personality characteristics that strengthen and enhance their being. Those are the bases around which most people get to know each other and through which future relationships are built. The younger years are often thought to be the times that friendships are developed, but as people live longer, they find new opportunities and circumstances that lend themselves to new relationships. A move to an older-adult community, enrolling in a class, participating in a discussion group or other activity, or attending programs at local community centers provide a background for new acquaintances and friends, some of which will be enduring. Many older adults find that they rediscover friends that they have not seen in years, when their paths cross, and there is a chance for a reunion. Friendships are crucial to later life, and considerable effort should be spent to start new ones and nurture and maintain long-standing relationships.

Most older adults, and even most in the middle years, have few, if any, friends who are more than a decade younger in age. Over the years, many of these contemporaries are lost to relocation, illness, and death. Having a more diverse network of acquaintances and friendships of varying ages offers some buffer from that loss. In addition, those who are vitally involved with life, in Erikson's terms, may find that having younger friends, with possibly different views of life and different interests, can be refreshing and stimulating. For the younger people, older adults can bring wisdom, experience, and a sense of history and perspective that are difficult to have at age 25, 30, or even 40. Older friends may be valued as auxiliary or surrogate parents who are appreciated for their support and understanding, when parents have died or are not as capable of support and understanding.

Those who complain about loneliness may initially reject the idea of doing anything about it. The availability of someone to make initial telephone calls for information about activities or provide company for the first visit to the community center sometimes is needed, for even the most competent older person may feel lonely and vulnerable. Older people should periodically take stock of their lives with regard to their activity schedule and habits. Each individual has a personal tolerance for time alone, for activities, and for desire to be with others but nevertheless should ask some questions periodically: Am I racing around so much that I have almost no time to relax? Am I spending too much time alone? Are there things that I do alone that I might enjoy with others? Shopping, exercising (even taking a walk in the neighborhood), and going to a concert, play, or movie can be done alone or with one or more friends or acquaintances. Book and discussion groups and informal social activities for adults of varying ages are available in most communities.

For many people whose lives had revolved around work for decades, leaving it, even for a well-planned retirement, can be uncomfortable; for others, it can be lonely or even traumatic.

Many parts of the business community are showing a growing interest in hiring and rehiring retired workers and in encouraging potential retirees to continue working part time. Because of the increasing shortage of people in the work force and because mature people can be dependable workers, often with well-developed skills, older adults will do well to consider working as an alternative to full retirement. Retired professionals and business-people in the Service Corps of Retired Executives

(SCORE), a federal program administered by the Small Business Administration, supply their expertise in local programs to help younger people get started or solve problems in their business situations.

Because there are fewer younger women available to serve in volunteer capacities in the community, older men and women are welcome, and indeed crucial, to provide services that were previously performed by younger housewives. Vital voluntary positions in schools, social agencies, religious, charitable, and political organizations, and community programs are unfilled because more younger women are working for pay than ever before and retired older people have not thought to serve in these capacities. The Retired Senior Volunteer Program (RSVP), a federally sponsored volunteer program specifically for older adults, operates through local groups throughout the country and serves as a clearinghouse for appropriate and useful volunteer positions. Through volunteer efforts, older adults fulfill needed roles in the community and open up opportunities for socialization and potential friendships for themselves. Many cities and towns have well-developed peer counseling and peer support projects, in which older people learn how to work with others in their age range, around common concerns and difficulties. These programs have been extremely beneficial to both the people counseled and the counselors, who achieve an expertise and a feeling of camaraderie for the rewarding work they do.

Contrary to a popular stereotype, older people can learn new information and develop interpersonal and other skills. Colleges and universities offer continuing education programs for older adults, and at many schools older people may audit day classes at little or no cost. These are opportunities for personal growth and serve as environments for starting new relationships. One 77-year-old man learned bridge with a group at a local library. He had never been gregarious and had never sought out other people just for companionship. He attended the twice-weekly bridge sessions "for intellectual stimulation" and found, to his surprise, that he also enjoyed the social times before and after the cards were dealt, "in spite of himself." Through his interests in books and bridge, he met and became friendly with people who were twenty to forty years younger than he. He marveled at his ability to have common interests with "youngsters" and soon discovered they were friends on whom he could rely.

The issues of loss, loneliness, and bereavement accentuate a tendency to think of older adults as weak, disabled, and vulnerable. Some are. But the majority of older people are resilient and capable and, with some assistance and support, are able to recover from a loss or period of loneliness to continue to lead a full life, albeit with residual pain. Perpetuating a negative stereotype results in a societal belief of incompetence that is destructive to the older victims and also to younger people who witness this. Times of crisis, loss, and grief allow us to see ourselves and our older friends and relatives in great pain and acute distress. Those are usually temporary states from which we will rebound, sometimes with "a bit of a limp."

4

Sleep: More or Less

The worst things:
To be in bed and sleep not,
To want for one who comes not.
To try to please and please not.
—Egyptian proverb

Sleep is a vital part of our lives. We spend about one-third of our lives sleeping, and it very much affects mood, productivity, and general quality of life. Sleep and its associated disturbances are among the most common topics and complaints of people as they age. "I was up all night"; "I didn't sleep a wink"; "I tossed and turned all night" are frequent refrains. Indeed, the character of sleep changes substantially with normal aging; few people sleep as well as they did when they were younger. The long hours of sleep of the infant and the deep sleep of the adolescent are envied by those who can have neither the long nor the deep.

Sleep is measured in length of time, in depth, and in terms of intercurrent events, such as dreams, body movements, awakenings, snoring, and changes in breathing patterns. It is affected by noise and comfort of the environment, psychological state (such as anxiety, depression, and dementia), medical illness, pain, medications, alcohol, eating patterns, exercise, and daytime activities. All of these affect a person's perception, and the reality, of having had "a good night's sleep." Normal older people sleep less well than they did as younger adults, and they are more vulnerable to environmental and physical changes that affect sleep. Despite these difficulties, sleep for most people can still fulfill the function of restoration without excessive daytime sleepiness. Although sleep has been a subject of intensive study for decades and much has been learned about its physiology, it and the accompanying dreams still remain a mystery. The functions of sleep are presumably homeostatic, providing balance and restoration to the brain and body functioning. While people vary in their needs for sleep, from five to nine or more hours out of twenty-four, it is known that chronic sleep deprivation from the usual pattern may cause irritability, depression, irrational thinking, and other physical consequences. Interestingly, acute sleep deprivation has been used as an experimental treatment for severe depression, although it has its limitations as a long-term therapy.

Because of advances in the field of sleep research, clinical sleep assessments and staging and accurate diagnosis of sleep difficulties are possible. The technique of polysomnography measures brain electrical activity with an electroencephalogram (EEG), as well as tracking eye and limb muscle movements and the regularity of breathing patterns. This evaluation is usually done in a sleep laboratory, which consists of a noise-free room with a comfortable bed, a one-way mirror, and various monitoring machines. After having a number of leads (wires) attached to parts of the scalp, face, and limbs, the subject gets into the bed and goes to sleep. The wires are attached to a machine that plots brain waves, eye and limb movement, and other physical functions. From these measurements, over the course of a period of sleep, descriptions of sleep characteristics can be made.

Throughout the night, sleepers move through a course of various sleep stages. Sleep is generally divided into rapid eye movement (REM) and non–rapid eye movement (NREM) periods. The latter is subdivided into several stages, from light (stages 1 and 2) to deep (stages 3 and 4). Sleep is regulated in several parts of the brain and affected by several of the neurotransmitters—serotonin, norepinephrine, and acetylcholine—present in those areas. Neurotransmitters are specific brain chemicals that facilitate activity among the neurons that make up the brain. The sleep-wake cycle is a function of the circadian rhythm, which is regulated by the brain.

Changes in Sleep with Normal Aging

Older adults have a range of daily sleep time from five to nine hours, similar to younger people. Each individual has a customary sleep time, which provides enough rest to allow the person to function during the subsequent day. In older adults, sleep time is often divided between short daytime naps and a somewhat longer period of night sleep. Explorations of abnormal sleep patterns consider four questions: (1) What is "normal" sleep for the individual in question? (2) Is the person satisfied with the quality of the sleep? (3) Does the bed partner or roommate complain about the person's abnormal sleep patterns or behavior? (4) Does sleepiness affect the person's daily schedule of activities?

Research has demonstrated that although older people probably spend as much time sleeping as they did when they were somewhat younger, it is less efficient and may be less satisfying. The sleep of older people is shallower than in earlier years; they experience a decrease in the amount of deep (slow wave) sleep and more very brief periods of awakening during sleep than do younger people. The major sleep period occurs earlier in the night. They have more changes from one sleep stage to another during a night's sleep and are more likely to awaken early. Daytime napping time and total time spent in bed are increased. Older people snore more and have periods of decreased respiration during sleep, sometimes including sleep-disordered breathing episodes, with very brief periods of respiratory cessation (apnea). Because older people have more disrupted sleep compared to younger adults and because of the relationship between sleep and a general sense of well-being, sleep and the lack of it can become major preoccupations of older people. Sleep complaints generally fall into two categories: problems falling asleep or staying asleep at night, and specific problems with daytime sleepiness. Two other less common problems are disorders of the sleep-wake cycle (circadian rhythm) and sleep-related disorders such as sleepwalking, sleeptalking and disturbing dreams.

Sleep Assessment

Because more than half of all older people have some sleep complaints, many accept sleep disturbance as a part of growing older and either suffer with it or obtain medication in an attempt to treat it. Few people seriously approach their sleep disturbances with a physician as a health problem, except when they become extremely disabled by the difficulty. Sleep disturbances have been frustrating to treat, but the advent of new diagnostic and therapeutic techniques makes them more understandable and easier to manage.

The sleep assessment by a physician begins with a history of the problem. The history is best obtained from the patient and, if possible, corroborated by the person who sleeps closest to the patient (in the same bed, room, or house). Everyone has periods of days or a few weeks in which sleep is less than optimal, and this is usually caused by an acute illness or a transient environmental, situational, or psychological problem. In older people, the distinction between sleep changes associated with normal aging and those of a true sleep disorder must be considered. A log kept by the patient and/or bed partner over two to three weeks, detailing the time of sleep and disruptions in it, is helpful in understanding the nature of the problem. Sometimes a spouse can make an audiotape recording of the patient's sleep noises. This may add valuable information to the assessment process.

Medical and mental health histories and examinations are important to obtain. The dietary history should focus on the eating pattern during the day and on stimulating foods, such as those containing caffeine and alcohol. (Many beverages, such as sodas and other canned drinks, contain caffeine.) Total fluid intake, particularly late in the day, is relevant because the need to urinate during the night may cause wakefulness and disturbed sleep. A history of medication use for all disorders is crucial, including over-the-counter drugs and particularly, drugs used to treat insomnia. Exercise and activity patterns are useful pieces of information in the evaluation of a sleep disorder. If the sleep disorder is short term—a few days to a few weeks—the physician will focus on situational or transient causes. If the insomnia is more chronic, a sleep study in a sleep laboratory is helpful in making a diagnosis.

Problems Associated with Falling Asleep or Staying Asleep

Insomnia is the problem of falling asleep or staying asleep on a regular basis (at least three times per week, for at least a month). Trouble falling asleep can be due to a multitude of causes, but many older people complain of insomnia as a primary and isolated problem, with few associated physical or emotional complaints. Most people who do not sleep well become quite anxious and frustrated about the prospect of continuing insomnia. Some older people who report chronic insomnia, lasting several decades, find ways to accommodate to the disorder.

Environmental disturbances, such as poor sleeping conditions, noise, odors, temperature, light and eating, drinking, and medication patterns, can cause insomnia. Recent moves, changes of bed furniture, or changes in the people in bed or in the room may be significant. Activity level, timing of exercise, and dramatic changes in life-style may affect sleep. People who are sedentary during the day sleep less well at night.

People with psychiatric problems—anxiety, depression, mania, or dementia—may have difficulties initiating sleep and staying asleep. Anxious patients are more likely to have difficulty falling asleep, and depressed patients generally complain about early morning awakening, but these generalizations are frequently reversed. People suffering with dementia may be agitated and confused and have grossly disordered sleep patterns, probably due to organic factors and environmental issues.

Any acute and chronic illness, particularly those of the cardiopulmonary system, may make it difficult to initiate and stay asleep. Heart disease and emphysema may cause respiratory distress, which worsens in a reclining position and may result in multiple awakenings "to catch a breath." Painful arthritis, "heartburn," and low back pain make continuous sleep impossible. Men with prostate enlargement may experience multiple awakenings to urinate. Most older people make at least one nighttime trip to the bathroom. Older adults who are grieving, particularly after the loss of a spouse, may have symptoms of insomnia for a year or more after the death.

Problems Associated with Daytime Sleepiness

When a person complains of daytime sleepiness, there is an implication that sleep is unsatisfactory in some way or there is some illness or disorder that affects daytime wakefulness directly. Those who experience true daytime sleepiness (hypersomnia), caused by a sleep disorder, usually cannot stay awake during daytime activities, such as work, recreation, and social events or meals; they are more than just somewhat tired or fatigued. Most people with daytime sleepiness may be unaware that they are sleeping poorly during the night; they know that they cannot stay awake during the day, however. Other than the problems of obtaining grossly inadequate nighttime sleep for one of the reasons discussed above, the most common causes of daytime sleepiness are sleep apnea, periodic leg movements, and medical, neurological, and psychiatric disorders.

Sleep apnea is a common problem diagnosed by sleep specialists in older people with daytime sleepiness. In this disorder, a person has multiple, sometimes hundreds, of brief awakenings caused by breathing pauses of fifteen to forty seconds in length. Increased breathing disruptions produce increased sleep disturbance and increased daytime sleepiness. People who are afflicted with this problem are rarely aware of the sleep disturbances, although their bed or room partner will hear them snore and stop breathing repetitively during the night. Sleep apnea may be due to a central respiratory problem in the brain or a more common local obstructive problem. In the latter, the airway, particularly in obese people, in the back of the throat and neck may be relatively impeded by excess tissue in the throat and neck, or the airway may collapse because of relatively relaxed tissue in the neck. In the most severe forms of sleep apnea, patients are chronically deprived of oxygen and become confused, have difficulty concentrating, and evince personality changes, including withdrawal, depression, and intellectual impairment. Other symptoms are headaches, impotence, and urinary difficulties.

Sleep apnea responds dramatically to treatment. Initial treatments might include weight loss, if obesity is thought to be a factor, or treatment with certain antidepressant medications that improve mild symptoms, probably by altering sleep depth and snoring patterns. The use of tranquilizing or sedative medications for people with sleep apnea is specifically contraindicated; they can impair breathing ability and be life threatening.

The most frequently used treatment for moderate to severe sleep apnea is nasal continuous positive airway pressure (CPAP). The patient wears a tightly fitted mask over the nose at night, through which a continuous flow of air is delivered through a tube from an air compressor. Essentially the patient is constantly supplied with air under pressure sufficient to keep the obstruction from blocking the patient's airway during sleep. Although the device is somewhat cumbersome, the treatment quickly eliminates all symptoms of sleep apnea, and most patients accept this treatment in lieu of surgery to remove excess tissue in the back of the throat, including tonsils, adenoids, the uvula, and part of the soft palate. This surgery relieves snoring and sleep apnea 50 to 75 percent of the time. Nasal speech and regurgitation of food are possible but infrequent side effects. Another surgical procedure, performed in extreme situations, is tracheotomy, which bypasses the obstruction in the throat. The use of CPAP has significantly changed the prognosis of this disabling disorder, without invasive intervention.

Periodic leg movements (nocturnal myoclonus) is a common sleep disorder in which the patient suffers multiple leg muscle contractions or jerks that result in daytime sleepiness. These may occur in clusters during the night, accounting for several hundred bursts of activity. The multiple awakenings obviously result in daytime sleepiness. Bed partners report that the patient moves his or her legs excessively at various times during the night. The treatment for this problem is a benzodiazepine, usually clonazepam (Klonopin); it may not decrease the movements but will decrease the patient's awareness of them and also decrease the wakefulness during the night.

Various medical disorders that affect the heart, lungs, kidneys, and liver may cause daytime sleepiness, as can the medications used to treat many medical problems. Neurological conditions and psychiatric problems of the elderly, especially depression and dementia, may be factors in sleep disturbances. Treatment for any of these should be directed at the underlying cause.

Other Sleep Disorders

Sleep-wake cycle disturbances occur most commonly in shift workers and in jet lag. The cycle is said to have a phase advance, when sleepiness occurs earlier in the evening, and phase delayed, when it occurs later. Normal older people occasionally experience sleep cycle disturbances that can be treated behaviorally, with increasingly later bedtimes, and in the short term with benzodiazepines. The use of bright light therapy may prove to be an effective treatment for sleep cycle disorders. Sleep-wake cycle disturbances are common in demented patients. Up to two thirds of residents in long-term care settings have significant sleep problems.

Problems such as sleepwalking (somnambulism) are more common in children and young adults than in older people. Many demented patients awaken during the night and wander, although this disturbance is not considered true somnambulism. This is a significant management problem because seriously impaired people may injure themselves or leave the house (see chapter 10).

Treatment Issues

Aside from the specific treatments for sleep apnea and periodic leg movements, the treatment of insomnia, particularly the problems in initiating and staying asleep for the night, is challenging and often frustrating for elderly patients and their physicians. There is considerable variation in sleep time and sleep quality in older adults, so the first step in the process of treating insomnia is to ascertain that a sleep disorder exists. Then education is required. Sleep schedules and characteristics are different in older people, and some adjustments may need to be made; some degree of insomnia may be chronic and tolerable.

Sleep specialists speak about the value of good sleep hygiene as a first-line treatment for insomnia. It encompasses scheduling regular bedtimes and wake-up times; having a quiet, comfortable sleep environment; doing regular exercise early in the day; avoiding caffeine, particularly after noon; avoiding alcohol late in the day; reducing nap time; using the bedroom only for sleep and sex; limiting time in bed to actual sleep time; making good use of nonsleep nighttime when others are sleeping; and, if stressed or worried, spending 15 to 30 minutes thinking about and writing down worries, early in the evening.

Medical, neurological, and psychiatric disorders and chronic pain that might interfere with sleep should be maximally treated. Medications, alone or in combination, for the treatment of non-sleep disorders should be assessed to ensure that they are not factors in causing insomnia. Small amounts (four to six ounces) of warm milk, herbal tea, relaxation techniques, meditation, and other nonpharmacological treatments that individuals find helpful should be tried.

What about medications for sleep? Most sleep specialists agree that sedative-hypnotic medications should be avoided, except when there is an acute medical or psychological problem or a life crisis, and then only for a few days to two weeks. In practice, many people take short-acting benzodiazepines to induce and maintain sleep, when behavioral treatments have failed. Triazolam (Halcion), temazepam (Restrol), and lorazepam (Ativan) are the most commonly prescribed benzodiazepines for sleep. They should be used in the smallest possible dosages in older patients. They are very short to relatively short acting and are effective sedative-hypnotics but have potential adverse effects that must be considered when embarking on a course of treatment. Chief among these are potential habituation with tolerance—the need for increasing dosages. Other side effects are "hangover" effects, amnesias, confusion, rebound insomnia (when the drug wears off too soon), depression, and anxiety. There is no place for barbiturates in the treatment of sleep disorders in the elderly. They are addictive, lethal in overdose, and may cause confusion and depression.

If medication is required to treat insomnia in older adults, particularly when depression is present, others drugs are also available, including sedating antidepressant drugs such as trazodone (Desyrel) and amitriptyline (Elavil) and diphenhydramine (Benadryl) and chloral hydrate (Noctec). The benefits and adverse effects of these must be considered (see chapter 9). Nonprescription, over the counter, medications usually contain sedating antihistamines. They should be used cautiously and in consultation with a physician.

Despite recent significant gains in the understanding of the physiology of normal sleep and the patterns of sleep disorders, the treatment of sleep difficulties is still in its infancy. The older population presents complicated challenges in understanding the relationship between sleep problems and the changes associated with normal aging, medical and psychiatric disorders, medications, and changes in neurotransmitter function in healthy aging and disease. Because sleep disturbances are so common in the older adult population and because the treatments for many cases of insomnia are inadequate, there is a need for significant research effort in this area. That work is in process.

5

Sexual Life after Seventy

Sex doesn't help you live longer,
but it may make you want to.
—*Anonymous*

Sex is a difficult subject for older people to talk about, and it is even more difficult for others to talk about with older people. The 75-year-old woman mentioned in chapter 1 who "thinks about sex almost daily" and an 82-year-old man I know who expresses surprise, even outrage, that someone would consider him "too old" to be and feel sexual are more outspoken than most although not otherwise atypical of older people who are enjoying active sexual lives. But as with all other issues concerning older people, the diversity among them is greater than in any other age group. Some feel happy to have fewer sexual expectations put on them because they never liked sex much anyway, and in the later years "it's even more of a burden." Some are less interested in intercourse than in the past but enjoy the holding, kissing, touching, and caressing that convey love and caring. Some men have more trouble with erections than earlier in their lives but yearn to have sexual experiences as they did in the past. Other men are afraid to think or talk about sex because they do not want to be considered "dirty old men." Some women feel very sexy but think it is unseemly to be too aggressive; many have trouble finding men who are interested or loving. Some women remember earlier days with a smile or a tear and feel good that they had been with men who cared so much for them. And some people still enjoy sexual experiences much the same way they did in the past, sometimes better, or somewhat worse.

Sexuality is one of the least discussed subjects after adolescence; indeed, geriatric sexuality is viewed by most people, including medical and mental health professionals, as extremely limited or nonexistent and certainly not a subject to be discussed very much. When taking a medical history, physicians do not usually ask older people about their sexual life; they certainly do not ask older women. All concerned are embarrassed. Physicians do not always consider the effects of medications or other treatments on sexual activity as they would in younger people, and they are not responsive enough to sexual problems that patients may want to discuss. Precautions about sexual activity often are not mentioned after a heart attack, stroke, or other illness or surgery in an older patient, as they might be discussed with a 50-year-old. Older people see themselves, and often are seen by others, as asexual or at least as significantly sexually diminished. As one person put it, "When everything else is falling apart, how can you worry about sex?" And yet sex is an important part of a vital person; some might say that if "everything else is falling apart" and you can still enjoy sex, what better activity is there to have? Why not have it and value it as something that brings pleasure, a release from anxiety, and a feeling of being intact in a sphere of life that makes us feel alive?

Although there is diminished sexual activity with age, both men and women continue to have considerable sexual interest into the ninth decade. The subject of sexual interest and activity in older adults has not been well studied because of negative ageistic stereotypes, societal taboos, and physician-researcher-patient discomfort with the idea of the elderly as sexual people and because sex has often been narrowly equated with sexual intercourse. Sexual functioning actually changes relatively little with aging when compared to the diminution of other physical functions. Several studies show that one-quarter or more of people over 65 years of age abstain from an active sexual life for various reasons, but of the remaining people, the quality of sexual activity is as good as it was in younger years. Among those people who are sexually active, there is a decrease in sexual desire and frequency of sexual activity after age 75. In one study, up to 50 percent of married couples over 60 years of age reported having sex in the prior month, with a frequency of slightly more than four times per month.* In the group of people over 76 years of age, only 24 percent reported having sexual relations in the prior month. Other studies, including the Duke Longitudinal Study, report remarkably stable sexual interest and activity from middle to late life.† Men reported more sexual interest and activity than women, and men were also regarded more often as the ones responsible for cessation of sexual activity within a couple. Some couples report improved sexual functioning with age. They credit the absence of children, a decrease in day to day responsibilities, and more leisure time with their success. Most of the research in the area of sexuality in older adults has been focused on married couples; more needs to be known about the normal sexual practices of single, divorced, and widowed elderly, on homosexual life in the later years, and on the effects of illnesses and medications on sexual activity.

Changes in Women, with Age

Women mark the onset of "real aging" with menopause, although this usually occurs in their 40s or 50s. Menopausal changes occur first in the brain, the pituitary gland, and the ovaries, resulting in a cessation of the normal menstrual cycle and ovulation and a variety of other changes in the reproductive system and throughout the body. Some women experience few or no symptoms in the menopausal period; others experience anxiety, depression, decreased ability to concentrate, irritability, "hot flashes," sweating, and changes in sleep pattern. With the ovarian failure of menopause comes a decrease in the production of estrogen, which is responsible for maintaining the tissues of the female gynecological system. The vaginal muscles lose tone, and

*W. Marsiglio and D. Donnelly, Sexual relations in later life: A national study of married persons. *Journal of Gerontology* vol 46, No 6 S 338–334, (November 1991).

†L. K. George and S. J. Weiler, Sexuality in middle and late life, *Archives of Psychiatry* vol. 38: 919–923. (1981).

the tissues lining the vaginal wall are more fragile. The lubricating secretions produced in the vagina, normally and especially in response to sexual excitement, fall with decreases in estrogen levels. Because of hormonal changes, the skin, clitoris, and nipples may become more sensitive, and even painful, during sexual activity. The woman and her partner may find that they derive pleasure from different areas of the body and different kinds of sexually stimulating activity than they previously enjoyed.

Although their sexual desire may not be affected, women still must deal with the physical changes of normal aging. They may expect to be less desirable to men and feel less attractive. They may be less firm, with less general muscle tone, sagging breasts, and changes in hair color and character. As these changes occur, women may may have to adjust their self-image and deal directly, if they can, with their partners about their sexual expectations. The issue of self-image is heightened when a woman has had disfiguring illness or surgery. Some woman have difficulty coping with the youth and physical beauty marketing that is so much a part of our culture. Healthy, well-adjusted women can strive to value themselves as whole people, including the inevitable changes that aging might bring.

Changes in Men, with Age

Men may go through a form of menopause, the climacteric, somewhat later than women do. It is both a psychological and a physiological event. In aging men, there is less available testosterone, the predominant male hormone, and this decrease affects many of the changes in sexual functioning. The skin and muscle tissues of an aging man have less tone, and this may affect his general physical appearance and also the structure and function of his penis, the body part that most men associate with their sexuality. Because of changes in tissues, the penis of an older man may be smaller. A full erection takes longer to obtain, and the penis, when stimulated, may not be as hard as in younger days, although usually hard to enough to engage in intercourse. Men may require more stimulation, psychic as well as physical, to become fully erect. If they can relax, the longer time usually necessarily to achieve full erection brings older men (and women) the bonus of a longer period of sexual foreplay prior to ejaculation. Most men have a latency period of several hours before another full erection and ejaculation can be achieved. Older men may have less forceful contractions of the penis during ejaculation, and a smaller amount of semen is produced. The quality of the sexual response may be the same as at younger ages although somewhat less intense. Most older men adapt to these age-related changes and can have a satisfying sexual life.

Evaluating Sexual Functioning

If sexual functioning is valued as an important part of the relationship between two people or for the satisfaction of any individual, attention must be paid to problems that develop in maintaining an active sex life. But this is an area in which most people suffer in silence, attribute their abnormal sexual functioning to "old age," and never seek help. Although studies vary, approximately 50 percent of older couples have a sexual problem. Because an older person's sex life is even more private than his or her psychological state, those with sexual dysfunction must be extremely motivated to get help for themselves or do so at the insistence of their spouses. Physicians should include questions about sexual functioning as part of a routine history and physical examination of the patient. An evaluation of sexual functioning can be performed by a knowledgeable primary care physician, urologist, psychiatrist, or other mental health professional who is interested in this area of older adult life. A full evaluation may involve several of these professionals. The clinician must understand psychological and physiological functioning in normal aging, as well as the effects of medical illnesses, psychiatric disorders, medications, and life crises on the sexual life of the patient.

Most older adults are initially embarrassed talking about their sexual activities, particularly with a younger clinician, but they will shortly be relieved that someone is interested and that their sexual difficulties are taken seriously. The usual habits and patterns of sexual activity of the individual or couple should be noted. To what extent are the present complaints a change from the usual pattern? When did they begin? Were they of sudden or more gradual onset? Are there coincident acute or chronic medical, psychological problems, or stressful life crises, losses, or deaths? Have new medications been prescribed or dosages changed? Has either partner had recent surgery? Does the man ever have erections in the morning or during the night or when having sexual thoughts? What are the living arrangements of the person or couple? Is there privacy? Older people may complain of recent sexual problems or may at an advanced age complain of long-standing sexual problems.

> One 75-year-old man complained bitterly, for the first time in his almost fifty-year marriage, about how unsatisfying his sex life with his wife had always been. It had always bothered him, but now that he was retired and had fewer other physical and emotional outlets, it seemed even worse, and he sought help with his reluctant wife.

It is essential to evaluate the medical history with particular focus on diabetes and other endocrine problems, arthritis, cardiovascular, urinary, genital, vascular, neurological, and psychiatric disorders and any medications that are prescribed and taken for any medical problems. Sexual dysfunction can be an early symptom of any of these problems. The increase in symptoms associated with painful arthritis, chronic urinary tract infections, heart disease, cancer, and other conditions may drastically affect sexual desire and functioning. Alcohol intake, diet, and sleep patterns should be detailed because they may have an impact on sexual functioning. Treatment for enlargement or cancer of the prostate is frequent in older men. Depending on the type of treatment or surgical procedure, there may be changes in sexual functioning, including impotence and retrograde ejaculation, in which semen flows back into the bladder rather than out through the penis. New surgical techniques that are nerve-sparing and new medical treatments offer the possibility of minimal or no changes in sexual functioning. Before treatment for prostate and other genitourinary disorders is performed, patients should be informed about possible options, risks, outcomes, and adverse effects.

The routine physical examination should include the genital and pelvic areas to estimate the extent of changes secondary to normal aging and those that represent otherwise abnormal findings. In men, the groin should be examined for hernias or abnormal masses and the penis, scrotum, testicles, prostate, and rectal area examined for any significant changes. In women, the lower abdominal and groin areas should be examined and a complete genital and pelvic examination performed. Laboratory tests such as urinalysis, complete blood count (CBC), fasting blood sugar, thyroid function tests, and others are important. An estimate of cognitive functioning may be made by the administration of one of the many short screening tests, and a self-rating depression scale, such as the Geriatric Depression Scale (see chapter 9), may yield useful preliminary information about mental state.

There are situations such as resuming relationships, which include sexual intimacy, after the death of a spouse, or while a spouse is chronically ill, possibly demented, and residing in a long-term-care facility, for which an older person will seek help, because of feelings of guilt, betrayal, or continued sadness and mourning. These complex issues need to be sensitively addressed.

A 71-year-old man who had been widowed for almost two years developed a close friendship with a woman who wanted to be even closer. He had been faithful to his now-deceased wife for forty-nine years and had had no other significant prior sexual relationships. He still thought about his wife daily, and he missed her. He was anxious about the prospect of getting "too close" to his friend, although he was attracted to her and felt comforted by her companionship. "I feel like a teen-ager debating whether to 'do it' for the first time," he sheepishly admitted. He additionally worried about his long history of occasional impotence, which he felt that his wife had learned to deal with, "but no other woman would." With some encouragement from a counselor, he hesitantly discussed some of his feelings and concerns with his friend. To his amazement, she wanted to help him overcome his worries and would start by putting less pressure on him to commit to her.

A major depression or other psychiatric disorder may include or masquerade as a sexual problem. As part of any evaluation for a sexual complaint, a thorough assessment of mood and cognitive functioning should be made.

A 69-year-old woman brought her 69-year-old husband to their family physician because he had become completely disinterested in sex over the past year. He did not even want to be touched very much, something he had always enjoyed. Until approximately eighteen months prior to this visit, they had had an active and mutually satisfying sexual life; since then, it had progressively worsened. The man had complained of more pain from chronic arthritis and had seemed quieter during the past six months, but his wife had noticed little change in their routines. Both of them worked part time, and they had a variety of interests and activities, separately and together. She was worried that something was medically wrong with him, or perhaps he was having an extramarital affair.

The physician met with them together and then talked with the man alone. He examined the patient and took blood and urine samples for laboratory tests. In the privacy of the doctor's office, he admitted that he had been increasingly sad over the past year, had slept poorly, was worried that maybe he had cancer although he had no specific symptoms, and for no apparent reason felt hopeless about the future. His skin felt strange, and generally he felt as though he "had aged ten years in one." He was worried about himself but did not want to worry his wife. He thought that he had tried to be affectionate with her, although he definitely was not interested in sexual intercourse. After being satisfied that the patient had no physical disorder, the physician discussed the problem of depression with him. He agreed to see a psychiatrist.

A discussion and assessment of sexual function by a concerned clinician serves the important function of giving the patient permission to talk about what most older people regard as a taboo subject. It gives the physician information about the patient's sexual functioning, as well as yielding information about some aspects of his or her general medical and psychological health, activities, and relationships. It affords an opportunity for the clinician to educate the patient and to correct misconceptions and myths that are so prevalent in the area of sexuality and older adults. Finally, the assessment offers the opportunity for treatment of a usually treatable problem.

Specific Sexual Complaints

All of the sexual problems encountered by older people result from some interplay of age-associated changes and the additional factors already noted. An individual's desire for sex may be affected by these and by changes in specific hormonal levels brought on by aging. Assays of testosterone, luteinizing, and follicle-stimulating hormones can be performed. Testosterone replacement is possible and often helpful to many men who have low levels of this hormone. Androgen treatment for women has been used to stimulate libido.

The excitement phase of sexual response is where most of the sexual complaints in older people lie. The man's erection is less firm, and he may need both psychic and physical stimulation to obtain and maintain it. Anxiety about adequate performance may play a role in limiting the erection. The major difficulty that women have in the excitement phase is that of vaginal dryness and atrophy, caused by decreased estrogen levels, decreased sexual activity, or stretching due to multiple pregnancies or loosening of pelvic tissues.

The orgasm phase is the third part of the sexual response. Women generally report little change in quality and quantity or orgasms in the later years when compared to earlier experience. Men have a diminished response, smaller quantity of ejaculate, and a long refractory period between orgasms.

Treatment

At any age, openness, flexibility, good communication, and a generally positive relationship between two people increase the chances of a good sexual relationship and of overcoming the changes that result from aging and other periods of sexual dysfunction when they occur. A history of a satisfying sexual relationship earlier in life makes for a better prognosis when troubles arise later. Some couples overcome major chronic medical disabilities and great limitations in functioning because of their mature, mutually supportive relationship and their desire to maintain a pleasurable sexual life. Many must adapt their sexual activity to suit age-related and other changes in their physical status and maintain an intimacy and caring that is vital to a healthy relationship.

Sexual functioning can become the battleground for other marital or personal problems and the repository of hostility and unresolved conflicts, old and new, which are not otherwise discussed. In these cases, counseling or psychotherapy for the couple and/or the individuals can be useful to focus on the specific individual and marital issues and on the sexual problems in particular.

If the primary problems are in the desire phase, hormonal replacement, if indicated by low levels, may be useful. Since male testosterone levels are higher in the morning, sexual desire may be greater for them at that time, and couples may want to "schedule" their sexual activity more at those times. Most men have long refractory periods between orgasms and ejaculations and may have difficulty satisfying their mate's desires. They may be able to enjoy more frequent sexual experiences if they did not feel that intercourse or an organism was required on each occasion. In addition, if it is acceptable to both partners, the use of stimulating movies, reading material, and fantasy daydreams may be helpful. Sometimes nonsexual touching and caressing leads to greater desire.

In the excitement phase, where most difficulties arise, communication between partners is crucial but often ignored. Previous methods of stimulation might not work as well with increasing age, and both partners will benefit from talking about what is now pleasurable. The reassuring woman will help her mate feel more secure and supported when he has trouble obtaining and maintaining an erection. Sometimes her assistance inserting the partially erect penis into the vagina facilitates intercourse, and then a more complete erection may ensue. In rare situations where erectile problems are extreme, surgical procedures are available to insert a prosthetic devise in the penis to assist in erections. The woman whose hormonal changes affect sensitivity and vaginal secretions is helped by a considerate mate who learns what is gratifying to her and makes efforts to stimulate her appropriately. Estrogen replacement therapy should be discussed with the woman's physician to determine if it is appropriate. Estrogen creams or water-soluble jellies may be used to add lubrication when the vagina is dry. Women should urinate prior to sexual activity involving intercourse to avoid bladder and urethral sensitivity and pain. Rarely, changes in the pelvic structures, such as uterine and bladder prolapse, require restorative surgery for full function. Changes in the usual position during foreplay and sexual intercourse may facilitate excitement for both partners.

Specific sex therapy with a couple uses a combination of behavioral, cognitive, and supportive psychotherapy techniques. The problem area is defined and couples are given exercises to practice at home. These will be prescribed to increase the open communication and flexibility of the couple, as well as focus on the particular problem with which the couple presents. People who have a history of good sexual relating prior to the presenting difficulty have a better prognosis for success in sex therapy. Most of the current generation of elderly grew up in an era of considerable sexual repression and inhibition by today's standards. It is remarkable how often people grow up and old with little knowledge of genital anatomy—even their own, and certainly their mate's. They may not have adequately considered the need to talk about their sexual life with their mate, and they would rather sexually retire than make changes. They may not know what feels good or bad to their partner. Rigid sexual patterns of the past, which may no longer be satisfying in later years, may require adjustment. Talking about these issues may be relieving of long-endured anxiety and optimally will result in a more pleasurable sexual experience for both partners.

Homosexual Relationships

The homosexual experience is an area that is especially neglected in thinking about sexual functioning in older people. Many of the issues already discussed are pertinent, but there are some additional considerations. If sexuality is a taboo subject when thinking about older people, homosexuality is even more so, and yet an increasingly large group of people have grown old with partners of the same sex or, having previously been primarily heterosexual, have found pleasurable experiences, genital and otherwise, with partners of the same sex later in life. The close companionship, caring, and affectionate touching and holding that are vital parts of loving and sexuality may sometimes be satisfied in later life by same-sex partners, as well as in heterosexual relationships. Because of societal stigmas, homosexual couples may have a smaller or more homogeneous network. They may not get the support they need from a wider community or even from family members. They usually will not have had children nor grandchildren. They are usually close in age and will face similar stresses of aging together. They will have to deal with changes in sexual appetites and sexual functioning, and, ideally, have flexibility and maturity so that the changes and stresses of aging can be dealt with while the essence of their loving relationship is preserved.

Summary

Sexual functioning, whether narrowly defined by sexual intercourse or more generally viewed as a caring and loving companionship, is a valuable asset in the later years. It ideally includes aspects of sharing, supportive comforting, and mutual pleasuring that are vital, especially for those confronted by the crises and stresses that later life can bring. Sexual problems can be discussed, defined, examined, and successfully treated by competent professionals. Sexuality in the later years, no matter how it is defined, should not be minimized, trivialized, or made to feel dirty; rather, it should be perfected, refined, and adapted to suit changing needs and desires.

6

Better Living Places

A 70-year-old woman admitted that the four-bedroom house in which she lived and raised her children for thirty-eight years was too large now that her husband had died, and her children visited only occasionally. But she loved the house, she still knew many people in the neighborhood, and it didn't cost much to continue to live there. She felt able to take care of it. If she left, where would she live?

Most older adults prefer to continue to maintain their own homes; others desire changes that allow them to continue to have complete independence but perhaps in a smaller or less demanding setting. Most older people make their own choices about living arrangements, or do so in consultation with family and friends. More than 90 percent of people over the age of 65 years live in the community—either alone or with spouse or other relatives. Many older adults obtain supportive, medical, and personal care needs in the community—either in their own homes or in residential settings that are more like homes than institutions. Although elderly people fear the prospect of entering a nursing home, only 5 percent of people over 65 years of age actually live in nursing homes. Older people who need alternatives to completely independent living arrangements sometimes see the nursing home as an ominous prospect. They are frequently unfamiliar with the range of living situations that are available in most communities.

With the enlarging older population has come a rapid expansion of living arrangement opportunities: neighborhood residential buildings and suburban apartment, condominium, and townhouse complexes that allow only people over 55 to rent or buy; resort communities for older adults; senior citizen residences or congregate housing communities that provide a common dining area for some meals and minor nursing support; assisted-living, personal care, or domiciliary homes, which provide more social and medical support; various levels of nursing home care for mildly to severely disabled persons; and continuing-care and life-care communities, which provide a range of situations from completely independent apartments to nursing care, depending on the changing needs of the residents. Some or all of these kinds of facilities exist in most communities. In some resort areas of the country, there are heavier concentrations of retirement and older adult-related facilities from which to choose.

Some older adults balk at the notion of living in a homogeneous environment of older people. They prefer the more natural living environment of people across the age spectrum and at various stages of life. Staying in one's own home, or at least in a known neighborhood, may offer the opportunity to have neighbors who are just beginning their careers, have young families, or are in middle age and coping with some of the issues that older adults have recently faced.

A 73-year-old widowed woman who lived alone in the small house in which she raised her family was saddened that the street had changed so much. Her reliable neighbor across the street died of heart attack last year, and the elderly woman next door was taken to the hospital, and then a nursing home, with a fractured hip. It was sad to lose them, but she felt ties to her modest home, the tall trees that lined the street, and the mailman of twenty-five years. She had some new neighbors—a couple with a small baby on one side of her and some newlyweds across the street. She felt a sense of renewal and she wanted to be a part of it. She decided that she ought to paint the house "to freshen it up."

The older adult who is attempting to "age in place" (an unfortunate term, which has come to mean staying in one's non-institutional environment but connotes a sense of immobility or stagnation) is making a choice in which he or she minimizes the anxiety and disruption associated with moving, sometimes from a very well-known situation to a new one. Staying in one's home offers a sense of security to the older person. Existing and long-held homes can be architecturally modified and decorated to make them more suitable for older people. Kitchens and bathrooms can be modernized and plumbing and electrical systems upgraded. Steps can sometimes be turned into ramps and long-needed general repairs to furniture and structure made. Sometimes reorganizing or renovating the house to have a bedroom and bathroom on the first floor makes the difference between being able to manage at home rather than needing care in another setting. The costs of making such changes are usually far less than those of several years in an assisted-living or long-term-care facility. There are architects who specialize in design needs for older adults, and their consultations can be valuable in the attempt to stay in one's own home.

Assisted-living or congregate housing situations and the life-care or continuing-care environments have become popular and offer realistic opportunities for nearly "aging in place." These suit many people who want relief from the responsibility of their own house or apartment and the availability of nursing, social, or practical (meals, laundry, etc.) services on-site.

Relocating is stressful at any age; for older people it is especially complicated and even wrenching. It evokes feelings of loss of the familiar neighborhood, the family home, the place of many memories and events. For some, it means that this will be their last move. Some of the old furniture, pictures, and other cherished household possessions may have to be discarded. Boxes of old papers, books, and more memories must be gone through so that decisions can be made about what can be kept for a smaller house or apartment. A move of some distance means orienting to new neighborhoods, shops, services, people, and, possibly, climate. On the other hand, a move can be refreshing, liberating, and invigorating, if all the variables are carefully considered, trial visits are made to the new environment, and the people involved are flexible, healthy, and somewhat adventuresome. Sometimes a move is necessary because the older people can no longer properly care for themselves or their property. Any decision to move should be made with consideration of what changes would maintain or produce maximum functioning, physically and psychologically. If possible, a move and its implications should be carefully considered well in advance of the event and planned when life is relatively stable rather than soon after a major illness, death, or other catastrophe.

When an older couple or parent contemplate a move into the home of their children or grandchildren, all should be prepared for major changes in privacy, routines, and relationships. Schedules, responsibilities, and habits may need to be negotiated so that conflict is minimized. These issues should be confronted before the move, and preferably before significant discord is evident. There is a better chance of success in this arrangement if the family is not displaced from its usual living space, and the older person has private space within the home. Predictably there will be stresses and strains within the family as it adjusts to the new person, no matter how close the relationship. Adult children must not neglect their own marital relationship and the connections to their children while they support and care for the older person who has joined them. For young children, the experience of having a healthy older relative in their midst can be nurturing and supportive and provide a unique experience with a loving adult. If the older person is ill, demanding, or unusually interfering, strains within the family quickly become magnified and require attention. Sometimes a social worker or other experienced professional can help mediate difficulties. A three- to six-month trial period to explore the feasibility of the joint living situation is advisable; other options and contingency plans should be known to all concerned prior to the beginning of the trial period in case a destructive situation evolves. Then, while feelings will be bruised and guilt prevalent, alternate arrangements can be implemented more easily.

Any moves being promoted by family members should consider the absolute necessity of respect for the autonomy and welfare of the older adults involved. Adult children who become involved in their parents' decision to relocate can be easily caught in a dilemma between their parents' perceived needs and their own anxiety about the real or feared imminent changes in their parents' physical or emotional status. The feelings and resultant conflicts encountered by the older adults and their assisting family members and friends as they make these kinds of decisions have the potential to be explosive for all concerned and for their relationships. Changes in living arrangements can sometimes raise heated differences between adult children and their older parents or even between rivalrous siblings who either do or do not want to be responsible for parents' move and caring.

A 45-year-old man called to get advice about his 79-year-old parents. They lived in a city approximately 850 miles away in a home they had occupied for over thirty-five years. Certainly the neighborhood had changed over the years, and many of their friends had died or moved closer to their children or to warmer climates. But the older couple were content where they were, enjoyed relatively good health, and saw the recent family discussions about the possibility of their moving closer to their son as "ridiculous." Although the neighborhood had somewhat deteriorated, they knew many of the local merchants, attended a nearby church, and felt at home there. In their son's area, they would know only him and his wife; everything else would be foreign to them.

The son wanted to know whether he should "put pressure" on them to move. After a short discussion, it became apparent that the younger man was increasingly anxious about the possibility that his parents would have a significant illness or disability. It is true that it might be easier for him if they were closer if he, in fact, had to respond to their immediate needs. But what if they continued to be relatively healthy for the next five to ten years and continued to be able to take care of each other, as they had over the past? The son realized that his parents would be devastated by a move to a distant city at this point, and he focused instead on some options for helping them in their own home, if the need arose.

This is one kind of dilemma that arises around the issue of a move in later life. A rational approach takes into consideration the needs of the older people for the relatively near future and requires flexibility and respect for their independence. Each situation demands its own analysis by the older person(s) and any involved relatives, friends, and, if necessary, consulting professionals. The overriding theme of achieving or maintaining maximal functioning for the older people involved in the most independent life-style is a good guide, although it may at times conflict with what is most expedient for other family members. Adult children may have to cope with their understandable anxieties about their responsibilities in a way that allows them to be most helpful to their parents and relatives. If there are significant indications that people are in danger because of physical or psychological impairments or if the living environment is truly inappropriate to their level of functioning, other interventions may have to be suggested. Talking the matter through with a professional who works with older adults is often helpful to get new perspectives.*

All available options for the most independent living situation should be explored before more institutional solutions are examined. Sometimes, having a visiting daytime or live-in companion or relative solves many of the concerns and gives enough support, at least in the short term. Increasing an older person's daytime socialization and range of activities makes the living situation more realistic; an arrangement or person to provide transportation and facilitate the attendance at those activities is then needed. For more disabled people, employing a nurse or nurse's aide at home may prove to be a satisfactory plan. An adult day care center may be considered for its therapeutic and

*Vivian F. Carlin and Ruth Mansberg, *Where Can Mom Live?* (Lexington, MA: Lexington Books, 1987).

daily care benefits. A move to a well-staffed assisted-living residence can provide a comfortable living environment for all but the very ill. These residences come in many different varieties in terms of levels of comfort and sophistication of care. The assisted-living residence often bridges the gap, for a long time or forever, between living at home and living in a more institutional setting. Efforts should made to explore their existence in the community and to compare the "homey" qualities, the comforts, the staffing quality, the food, the availability of consultations, nurses, transportation to shopping, entertainment, and doctors' appointments among them.

Nursing Home Living

Nursing homes are for sick people. Even as recently as the early 1980s, nursing or convalescent homes were still considered places to which to move after retirement, to live out one's last days. That is no longer so. No one should go to a nursing home unless he or she is ill, recovering from an acute illness or surgery, in need of rehabilitation and nursing care after a hospitalization, or chronically ill and suffering from a mental or physical disability that precludes living in a less restrictive environment. The decision to enter a nursing home is sometimes made by an older person but usually is prompted by a family member, physician, or social service agency professional. The timing of a decision to enter a nursing home depends on the nature and extent of the medical or psychiatric problem, the ability and inclination of the spouse or other family members to care for a person at home, feelings about nursing home care in general and about specific facilities, the availability of a suitable nursing home bed, and financial considerations. Some vignettes make this point.

Mrs. G. is a 59-year-old woman who had been diagnosed with dementia, probably of the Alzheimer's type, about two years prior to a consultation sought by her husband. Mr. G., 62 years old and recently retired, needed some help coping with his wife's almost constant pacing and agitation and her unpredictable striking out. She lived at home with her husband, went to a day care facility on most weekdays, and was maintained on a changing regimen of medications, which were only partially effective. Mr. G. sought consultations with various physicians to find symptomatic relief for his wife. He was chronically exhausted but never stopped to think about the quality of his relationship with his wife or about the quality of his own life. He thought that they had some "good moments" together. He knew about the diagnosis of dementia but held out some hope that she might improve. He had little time and less energy for his own activities. He resisted any suggestion of nursing home placement because he felt he still wanted and needed time with her. He insisted he could manage the situation for now.

A 79-year-old man with severe emphysema lived alone in an apartment house for older adults. He rarely left the apartment, had necessary groceries delivered, but frequently was too weak to cook meals for himself. He was reluctant to give up his "freedom" but realized that he was losing weight, had little social interaction, and was lonely. Recently he had become incontinent of urine, primarily because he was "too slow getting to the bathroom." A visiting nurse suggested that he consider an assisted-living residence or nursing home where he could get nursing and medical care for his pulmonary disease, have meals prepared for him, and socialize with others. The incontinence was repulsive to him, and he agreed to visit several homes to pick one. A month after living in a nursing care center, he felt stronger and more buoyant, and his incontinence had remitted as he had a more consistent eating and drinking pattern and learned some techniques for behavioral control of his urinary problem.

Nursing homes can provide good care when other arrangements become unsatisfactory or untenable. In some clinical situations, nursing home care is the preferred course. Some family members feel too guilty and/or ashamed to admit that they cannot care or do not want to care for their loved ones. Two examples are pertinent.

A 55-year-old man brought his 80-year-old mother to see me for a consultation. She had been diagnosed with Alzheimer's disease five years earlier, and he wanted an evaluation of her current mental status. She was not at all oriented to the day, date, or year; she did not know in what city she lived, and she no longer recognized her children, grandchildren, or nurse. She spent most of each day sitting in a chair in her apartment, staring blankly and intermittently becoming very angry and abusive to her caretakers. She was incontinent of urine and stool. The man revealed that he was quite wealthy and provided his mother with private-duty nurses, but none of them stayed for more than five days and then another set was employed. The nurses complained that the family had unrealistic expectations of the mother and of the nurses' capacity to "make her better." Many of them were distressed by the extent of her deteriorated state.

Consultation with the family members dealt with their denial of their mother's state and the fact that she would get better care in a setting where nurses and assistants were trained to care for patients such as their mother. The parade of private-duty nurses who were not specifically trained to care for people as demented as their mother had not served her well; there was some evidence that she may have been abused by some of them. In spite of long discussions about the availability of good nursing home care in their community, it took many weeks to deal with their resistance, their guilt, and their shame.

Ms. B. sought consultation concerning her father's situation. He lived 250 miles away and was demented and depressed. He had lived in an assisted-living residence for several years but complained about the care he received. He wanted to move to his daughter's city despite the fact that he had a son and several family members who visited him regularly in his present location. His daughter worked full time, as did her husband; their children lived in distant cities. Ms. B. was clear that she did not want to be responsible for supervising her father's care; she had supervised the care of her now-deceased mother over an earlier five-year period. Now it was her brother's turn, even if she were better at it. If her father moved here, she would have to be his primary carer, and she was not prepared to be that. Ms. B. wanted to get support for her position and to get recommendations for living situations in her father's city. She accompanied him and her brother on a tour of several nursing homes and selected one that had an unusually high number of cognitively intact people. They met with a social worker and made the transitional arrangements. Ms. B. committed herself to visiting him monthly.

In addition to their primary roles as long-term-care facilities, nursing homes that are properly staffed and equipped can function as shorter-term rehabilitation places for patients with special needs after surgery, stroke, or medical illness when going home immediately from the hospital is not appropriate. As hospitals discharge patients more quickly after an acute illness or surgery, rehabilitative stays in nursing homes serve an important function. Stays may vary from a few weeks to six months, and care is focused on recuperation and recovery of function. Nursing services and physical and occupational therapies are important aspects of the short-term stay. Discharge planning should carefully consider the kind of living environment best suited to each individual.

Defining a Good Nursing Home

There are approximately 20,000 nursing homes in the United States. They are owned by for-profit corporations, not-for-profit organizations or groups, or religious organizations. They vary greatly in appearance, atmosphere, general quality, and cost. The task of finding a suitable nursing home for oneself or a relative should be undertaken with great care. People find out about particular nursing homes from medical and social work caregivers; from hospital personnel in the discharge planning process; from friends and relatives who have had experiences with nursing homes; from clergy; from local governmental offices on aging and consumer affairs; and from various voluntary organizations concerned with long-term care of the elderly.

Some of the decision making will be immediately affected by the appearance, environment, cleanliness, decor, and estimation of comfort that one assesses on a visit to the home. These are important to consider, but there are many other factors to be weighed. Federal accreditors of nursing homes that treat residents using Medicaid or Medicare funds use thirty-two key care and safety standards.* These standards offer guidelines that perspective residents and families can use in evaluating a nursing home for residence. Some of these can be observed on visits; others can be evaluated by talking with administrators, social workers, and admissions staff at the home and by checking with local governmental and voluntary agencies involved with the elderly and their care. The standards follow:

Abuse: Residents are safeguarded from mental or physical abuse.

Activities: There are programs of activities appropriate to the residents' interests, needs, and level of functioning.

Association: Residents are able to meet and communicate privately with others within the home.

Bed sores: Residents with bed sores get proper care to promote healing. Preventive measures should be instituted.

Catheter: Residents with urinary catheters get proper routine care and infection prevention. Attempts at behavioral control of urinary function should be made.

Change: Except in an emergency, residents are not transferred, discharged, or treatment radically changed without consultation with the resident or next-of-kin or sponsor.

Cleanliness: Living areas are clean and odor free.

Control: Residents with bowel and bladder control problems get rehabilitative training to encourage self-control.

Drugs: Drugs are given according to the attending physician's written orders.

*Victor Cohn, "Finding the Right Nursing Home," *Washington Post,* June 5, 1990.

Eating: Residents needing assistance with eating or drinking have those services available. Self-help devices are available for use by residents.

Emergency: Emergency medical care is available and provided when needed.

Equipment: Equipment used in resident care is maintained in clean and safe operating condition.

Food: Food is stored, refrigerated, prepared, distributed, and served under sanitary conditions. Food is presented in an appealing manner.

Funds: Personal funds of residents are fully accounted for by the facility.

Health care: According to a physician's instructions, a written health care plan is made by staff members for each resident.

Hygiene: Residents receive daily personal hygiene assistance to ensure cleanliness, good skin care, grooming, and dental hygiene. Individual preferences should be taken into account. Residents are encouraged to care for themselves, to the extent possible.

Isolation: Isolation techniques to prevent spread of infection are followed.

Linen: A quantity of linen is available to give proper care and comfort to residents.

Mechanical: Mechanical and electrical equipment is maintained in safe operating condition.

Menus: Menus meet each patient's nutritional needs in accordance with physician orders and recommended daily allowances.

Nursing: Nursing services are provided at all times.

Physician: The health care of each resident is under a physician's supervision.

Possessions: Residents may keep and use personal possessions and clothing as space permits.

Privacy: Residents are afforded privacy during treatments and care of personal needs.

Rehabilitation: Residents get rehabilitative nursing care to promote maximum functioning to prevent loss of ability to walk or move freely; attention is given to deformities and paralyses.

Restraints: Drugs to control behavior and physical restraints are used only when authorized by a physician for a specific time or in emergencies.

Rights: The facility ensures that written procedures for residents' rights are posted and followed.

Skin: Residents are given care to promote healthy skin and prevent skin breakdown.

Social/emotional: Services are provided to meet the residents' social and emotional needs.

Therapy: Physical therapy and occupational therapy are provided according to physician's orders by competent and qualified therapists and assistants.

Toilet: Toilet facilities are clean, sanitary, and odor free.

Treatments: Residents get treated properly with injections, intravenous fluids, colostomy/ileostomy, respiratory, and tracheotomy care, suctioning and tube feeding, when necessary.

A visit to the nursing homes being considered for residence will provide answers concerning various issues early in the application process:

Financial: What are the costs? the add-ons? To what extent does insurance cover the costs? What about Medicare and Medicaid insurance? What happens when money is depleted? Must the resident leave the home?

Atmosphere: Is the home welcoming? Are the common spaces attractively decorated, well lit, and clean? Can residents bring personal furniture, pictures, and other memorabilia? Do residents look content and well cared for? Is the dining room appealing? Is the food quality good? Does the staff seem professional in demeanor? Are they interested in and respectful of the residents? How do they handle a resident who is very upset?

Medical care: Is it provided by staff physicians or by private attending physicians? Is there an active medical director? What is his or her relationship to the other attending physicians? to consultants? What are the procedures for medical emergencies? What hospitals are residents taken to in emergency situations? Does the staff receive ongoing training on-site or through courses elsewhere?

Psychiatric care: Up to 75 percent of nursing home residents have some psychiatric diagnosis; dementia and depression are the most common. What is the availability of mental health consultations and treatment? Is a psychiatrist regularly on-site for diagnostic assessment and to advise on medications, psychotherapy, and family issues? Is there an adequate social work staff? Are their psychiatric nurse specialists available? Are there specialized units for the least and most impaired residents? How are they different? To what extent do residents appear drowsy or drugged? Are many residents in physical restraints? Are there other specialists readily available for consultation (dentists, podiatrists, audiologists, psychologists, ophthalmologists, ear, nose, and throat specialists, and others)? What physical therapy, occupational therapy, art, dance, and exercise specialists are available, and how often?

Activities: Is there consideration of the level of functioning in determining specific activities for specific people? Is there an active exercise program? Are residents encouraged to come out of their rooms to engage each other or a staff member? Are there chores, jobs that can be done by residents, much as they would if they were living in a more independent setting? What contacts does the home have with family members? Who is the primary contact person between the home and family? Are there regular family support meetings or groups?

The list is endless; each person and family will have individual issues to raise that go beyond those enumerated.

Because of the enormity of a move to a nursing home for all concerned, it is vital that the resident and family member feel as comfortable as possible with the decision and with the specific place that is chosen. A patient experiencing moderate to severe dementia may not understand the issues involved, and it may not be possible to discern the patient's feelings on the matter. Sometimes, particularly with a severely ill older person, the decision to enter a nursing home is made because the caregivers can no longer do the work that is now required, and the nursing home will provide better care. The family members assisting the perspective resident should ask themselves, "Is this a place in which I want my mother or father to live, and will I want to visit here?" The transition to a nursing home environment from a more independent living situation is stressful initially for both resident and family. Sometimes that decision is difficult for family members to make because of the guilt attached to it by many. "How can we put Momma into such a place?" some will say. And yet some of those places are caring and comfortable. The family should try to find one like that in their community.

The move to a nursing home almost always evokes a mixture of feelings of anger, guilt, sadness, fear, and relief among the various participants in the decision. Individual and family concerns and considerations in the nursing home admission decision should be discussed with a physician, social worker, or other professional knowledgeable about long-term-care issues. For everyone's sake, the family must stay involved with the resident and the home, during the transition and afterward. Residents in nursing homes generally receive better care when their family members and friends are actively involved with the home and have regular communication with the nursing home staff. Residents in nursing homes fare better when family members and friends visit and take them out for walks, auto trips, family events, entertainment, cultural activities, and shopping expeditions.

The place in which we live, at any stage of life, is of crucial importance to our being and our functioning. In later life, that may be even more significant because of the history of and long attachments to people, places, furniture, pictures, and other memorabilia and because this may be the last move for most of the people making it. Yet there is a danger that the importance of decisions about living places and moving will be minimized or trivialized by the older person and relatives, friends, or caring professionals or agencies. Any decision to relocate in later life should as much as possible focus on the question, "Is this a better place for me than I am now in, and why?" Older adults can often answer that question themselves and make the decisions necessary to effect changes. If they are not able to do so because of illness or mental incapacity and if they have left no instructions, those decisions should be made by others with the guideline, "Is this a better place for him or her to live?"

7

Planning for the Future

A 79-year-old businessman and writer was told that he may need heart surgery to correct a recently diagnosed aortic valve defect. The man was distressed not only because of the medical implications but because he had just embarked on a major writing project, "and besides," he said, "I have ten more years of work I want to do; you doctors have to figure that into the equation."

Ten years is a long time for which to plan. Most people, young and old, realistically have difficulty planning for more than three to five years into the future. With age, we become increasingly aware of the uncertainties of life, but as one patient of mine put it, "What if twenty years from now I'm still waiting for something uncertain to happen?" It is healthy to strike a balance between "living each day as it comes" and planning for the future. With some flexibility, plans that are made can be changed or revised to suit new situations and conditions. Not making plans can lead to great distress.

Many older adults stop planning for the future once they reach some point at which they consider themselves old. For some people that occurs at age 60, for others at 90, and for most it is somewhere in between. For some, the declaration of "old" occurs after surviving an illness, a heart attack, a stroke, or major surgery. They feel lucky to be alive, so in some ways they stop living. For some the onset of old age occurs after the death of a spouse. They may give up, no longer setting goals or making many plans, although they may have been extremely goal oriented during their younger years. They may be content "to just be," feeling that it is futile to make plans because of the uncertainty of their coming to fruition. They think that life has stopped for them or is going to stop at any moment, or they just do not want to think about the future because it appears so bleak. They may feel fortunate to have made it this long; so why not just accept one's age?

Some people do the opposite but with the same resultant lack of planning. They work hard to deny the fact that they are aging, live as though they were much younger, and fail to take even the minimal prudent measures to prepare for the future. They are often fortunate to have good health and stamina and not to have been reminded that even for them the clock ticks. Dwelling on the negative aspects of aging is demoralizing, but extreme denial of the inevitable course of one's life can be equally destructive. It allows one to forget to take some precautions and to make some plans, realistically and emotionally, that might allow better preparation for the process of normal aging. One man's story is a dramatic example.

Mr. B. is a 79-year-old athletic-looking man who appeared to be fifteen years younger than his stated age. He had retired from a business at age 68 and had spent ten years traveling to various places, visiting with friends, and enjoying a number of hobbies. He never focused on the fact that he was aging, and in fact he was extremely proud of his young appearance. He had no will or other legal documents in the event of disability or death. He was healthy and had not been to a physician since he needed some immunizations for foreign travel eight years ago. On a trip to California, he awoke one day in the intensive care unit of a hospital. He had been at a seaside restaurant with a friend and had "fainted." In fact, he had been taken to a hospital, and the diagnosis of a ruptured aortic aneurysm was made. He had had emergency surgery and on awakening found himself in bed with a number of tubes and wires attached to him and a respirator assisting him in breathing. He had a sinking feeling that life was, or was about to be, over. He thought that even if he got out of the hospital, he would never be the same.

He gradually recovered from the physical catastrophe, but six months later he was still deeply depressed that "his life was over." He was suddenly old! His denial had been dramatically shattered. Physically, he was completely well, but he felt that he could no longer function at the level he had for the past ten years, and if not, he "might as well be dead." He was hospitalized for treatment of depression.

All people who recover from a catastrophic illness have a period of physical recuperation and then a longer period of anxiety and worry about their vulnerability. They feel that they will never be the same, and to some extent they are right. Most people, however, cope with the uncertainty of their mortality and go on with their lives, in several weeks to months, in a pattern similar to what it was prior to the catastrophic event or in some reasonable alternative way. As they age, most people plan in some subtle, if not real, ways for the eventuality of a possible bad day. Mr. B.'s denial did not allow for the possibility of vulnerability, and he was devastated by the physical insult he suffered.

Older people, regardless of chronological age, physical condition, and spirit, need to plan for the future, good or bad. Having goals and making plans are realistic for most older adults in almost any condition. Plans and goals are essential to a sense of well-being. They can be longer term or shorter range, having to do with planning a trip, a special event, or an activity with a friend or relative. Goals and plans mean there is a future, and we have some role in determining aspects of that future. Not planning implies hopelessness and helplessness, feelings that are dangerous for people at any age but especially for the older person. Plans should be made for everyday things like the next meal or the next trip to the grocery store, for painting a room or the whole house or planting a tree, and for special occasions, for vacations, and for goals not yet achieved.

Plans encompass a will (most people do not have one, leaving state laws to determine the distribution of their estate), personal letters of instruction to heirs, power of attorney for financial matters, a living will or medical directive, a durable power of attorney for health care (sometimes these latter two are combined as an advance directive), and other legal and personal matters associated with possible disability and death. These should be completed once and reviewed periodically as life circumstances change or as laws concerning inheritance or medical-legal issues are revised. A close friend or relative should know the locations of these important documents, as well as birth certificates, passports, marriage certificates and divorce decrees, military records, deeds to properties and important possessions, insurance policies, and safe deposit boxes. Everyone has a future; not planning for it denies its existence and deprives the individual of some control over it.

An 80-year-old man took full responsibility for the care of his 82-year-old wife, who had had multiple strokes and was concerned what would happen to her in the event of his disability or death. They had no surviving relatives. With the assistance of a younger friend, he made advance arrangements with a nursing home that agreed to take the wife as a resident on an emergency basis, if the need ever arose. He separately arranged for the friend to serve as a financial executor.

After the death of her husband, a 73-year-old woman realized that having been his caregiver and nurse for the five years prior to his death, she had missed out on some of the enjoyment that she had hoped for in her retirement. Except for some problems with arthritis and chronic indigestion, she was in good health and felt vigorous. She enrolled in a local college's continuing education program for afternoon classes in art and literature, two areas that interested her but which she had never studied. She joined an organization that sponsored low-cost travel. She hoped to be able to take one or two trips each year in the United States. These plans helped her cope with her loss and to fulfill some goals that she had set during her many busy working years.

A fully competent, gregarious, although somewhat frail 93-year-old woman had numerous opportunities for visits with relatives and old friends in several cities. For every major holiday, there were a variety of family activities planned with her children, grandchildren, and great-grandchildren. During the summer, three friends, each in a different location, wanted her to visit for several weeks, and during the winter she had traditionally gone to Florida for a month or two. She disliked planning to go but loved the actual travel, although it was tiring. Before each venture, she would try to get someone to say that she should not go. She worried about getting sick in another city and about being a burden to her hosts; she would procrastinate about getting ready and packing, leaving her apartment, and making arrangements for her cat. "Maybe I'd just do better at home," she would say. In fact, she was bored at home; she wanted more excitement and liked being with people. One day, in exasperation, a friend said, "Mary, you are afraid to plan anything because you are always waiting to drop dead. Think how many things you would have missed out on in the last ten years, if you had just stayed home waiting to die!"

Each of the individuals in the three vignettes needed or wanted to plan different aspects of their future and benefited from that planning in different ways. The gentleman had administered the care of his wife for several years and wanted to ensure her good care in case he died or was disabled. The knowledge that he had made contingency arrangements allowed him to be at ease about that responsibility in his later years. The vital 73-year-old woman had devoted five years to the care of her husband. Although she missed her husband, she was healthy and vital and she yearned for a full life in retirement, and planned it carefully. The 93-year-old woman was ambivalent about her status. She had trouble believing that she could still enjoy her interests, activities, and social functions. She saw all of her immediate contemporaries die and had to guard against just waiting for that to happen to her. With the support of her friends, she was able to keep planning her busy life.

Retirement

Retirement is an opportunity for major planning efforts by middle-aged and older adults. Most people retire voluntarily, and most are in their early 60s. There is much reason to think that a voluntary retirement will be successful, with no significant physical or emotional consequences. Since people in the United States spend more than 20 percent of their life in retirement, decisions about how and when to retire must be made thoughtfully. Older adults who have compelling avocations, activities, hobbies, specific retirement plans, or the drive to develop these do particularly well in retirement. Planning and continuing to set goals for how to spend retirement years are crucial. Increasingly, employers, social service agencies, and organizations interested in the welfare of older people (the American Association for Retired Persons (AARP), National Council on the Aging (NCOA), and other local governmental and voluntary agencies) offer information, courses, and programs for retirement planning. The process of thinking through a tentative, modifiable plan is useful for its own sake and for its function in decreasing anxiety about a major life change.

Retirement often brings an initial period of relief, a honeymoon, in which the older person feels "so lucky to have all this time." In three to nine months, a period of letdown may occur when the retiree thinks that life is more boring and unfulfilling than it used to be. A period of reevaluation and resetting of goals may be necessary. Since retirement can be a way of life for twenty or more years, there are repeated opportunities to change activities and life-style. For some people, the gratification derived from career or job, paid or volunteer, is crucial to feelings of worth and well-being. For many, it makes sense to approach retirement in a graded, flexible way, with gradual changes in work schedule over several years. For some older people, particularly those with resistances to establish new goals, complete retirement is to be avoided or contemplated only with much structure.

> A 76-year-old recently retired attorney became despondent when he realized that he "wasn't doing anything since he retired." He spent the morning reading two newspapers, taking a walk, and sometimes shopping. Twice during the week he played tennis, and he met a friend for lunch at a downtown restaurant one day each week. Since the age of 16 he had been a hard-working, striving man who always had goals, primarily school and then work oriented, that challenged him. Now he had none, and he felt useless. "I'm not doing enough," he said. After casting about for some activities of interest "that were not just busy work," he became involved in a mediation project at the city courthouse. He had responsibilities to clients and to the court but the flexible hours he wanted.

The importance of volunteer work and the development of avocations in the middle and later years, especially in preparation for retirement, is mentioned in chapter 3. Volunteering is not only beneficial for the various community, religious, educational, and other agencies that need the skills and expertise of a cadre of mature people, but, in addition, the individual continues to use his or her talents in a productive and meaningful way. The personal benefits of camaraderie and socialization are also significant.

Other critical issues to be faced in contemplating retirement include economic considerations, housing, possible relocation, and effects on spouse and adult children. Having enough money, living in a comfortable environment, and being able to enjoy the companionship of family and friends are factors that help make retirement a positive experience and increase the chances that it will be successful.

The Age Discrimination in Employment Act (ADEA) prohibits a mandatory retirement age for workers in the United States, except in occupations, that are particularly physically demanding, such as police or firefighting. Although most people will continue to retire in their 60s, a small but growing number of people will continue to work into their 70s and 80s. These people, largely in white-collar positions, are more evidence of the diversity in the older population and demonstrate ways in which healthy, competent people can continue to fulfill career goals, particularly where, because of personality, the nature of their work, or lack of other interests, work is essential to self-esteem and happiness.

Retirement offers an opportunity, but it can become a period of incarceration and boredom if not well considered and planned. One's personal work, activity, and emotional histories are crucial aspects of life to examine. One's personality, life-style and those of a spouse or other significant people in life should be thoughtfully considered. And the practical matters of finances and living space must be reviewed. Most people do it well.

Advance Directives

There has been increasing attention paid to everyone's right to be better informed about and involved in decisions about health care. We are all encouraged to ask physicians and other health care providers about the necessity for and interpretation of examinations and laboratory tests, as well as the risks and benefits of medications and other treatments. That is good advice. Adults who are not mentally disabled have the right to decide whether they want a particular, or any, medical treatment. Following on this idea is the importance of being involved in decisions about health care and life-sustaining treatments, in particular, at a time in the future when we may no longer be able to express our wishes.

Advance directives (living will, durable power of attorney for health care, or a combined document) are expressions by adults to give instructions about future health care wishes, in the event they are unable to express those wishes themselves. The case of Nancy Cruzan (*Cruzan* v. *Director, Missouri Department of Health* 1990), decided by the U.S. Supreme Court in June 1990, affirmed the right of a competent person to refuse life-sustaining treatment, including fluids and food, but stipulated that states may determine the proof required before a patient's wishes are followed. This case drew attention, as never before, to the issue of a patient's right to decide, in advance, what treatments he or she would want administered in a persistent vegetative or terminal state, at some time in the future. In October 1990 Congress passed the Patient Self Determination Act. As of December 1991, all health care facilities (hospitals, skilled nursing homes, home health care agencies, hospices, health maintenance organizations, and other health-related agencies) are required to inform patients of their rights to participate in health care decisions by using an advance directive document. The law was enacted with the hope that people, while competent, would define the extent to which they wanted life-sustaining and other extraordinary treatments at a later date. The law does not require that the patient execute any advance directive document. Rather, it requires that health care facilities provide adult patients, on admission, with written information concerning their right to accept or refuse treatment and the right to execute an advance directive, in conformity with state laws governing such matters. In addition, the facility staff must be educated about advance directives and their use so they can be of assistance to patients in their care. Documentation in the patient's chart must show whether an advance directive has been executed, and, if one has been signed, it must be verified as current. The facility cannot discriminate in the care of anyone on the basis of their execution of an advance directive.

All states in the United States recognize some form of advance directives. The most common are the living will, the durable power of attorney for health care, or some combination of these, sometimes simply referred to as an advance directive. Some states recognize the binding nature of a discussion of health care wishes between patient and physician, which is documented in writing. Others recognize informal notifications to family members. The living will lists various clinical situations that might arise in terminal conditions, persistent vegetative states, or irreversible comas, such as the need for mechanical respiration, cardiopulmonary resuscitation (CPR), amputation, tube feedings of food and water, pain medications, treatment of infections, and comfort care. The individual has the right to indicate, in advance, which treatments he or she might want and which are not desired, should a dire situation occur. The document can be changed at any time as long as the patient has the mental capacity to do so.

With a durable power of attorney for health care (in some states referred to as a health care proxy or agent), one designates an individual, usually a spouse, adult child, or friend, to make health care decisions on one's behalf in the event of incapacitation. The designated agent may be given specific or general instructions concerning future decision making on behalf of the relative or friend. Unlike the living will, which pertains only in terminal situations, the durable power of attorney may apply in any serious medical condition in which the patient cannot make a medical decision. Since not every clinical situation can be predicted, it is wise to give the agent guidelines (for example, on which life-sustaining treatments in a terminal condition or in the event of irreversible coma). This document, although often confused with a power of attorney for financial matters, is concerned only with health care decisions and only while the patient is not competent to make the decisions. A combined advance directive document appoints an agent or proxy and stipulates what treatments are desired in situations in which the patient may no longer be able to make those decisions.

Every healthy adult should execute an advance directive, designating someone who knows the individual's general wishes with regard to health care, to act in his or her behalf should he or she become incompetent. The document should stipulate as many of the specific situations that might arise. Simple forms are available that detail all of these and can be explained by lawyers, health care and social service agencies, hospitals, clinics and various organizations concerned with older adults (AARP; state attorney general's office; area agencies on aging; city, county, and state aging commissions). The legal issues in this field are still evolving, and the requirements for language, documentation, and witnessing vary from state to state. Before executing an advance directive, every person should check with local legal and/or health authorities to make sure he or she is in compliance with state law. A copy of an advance directive, when executed, should be given to the family member or friend named as the agent, to other concerned family members, and to the primary physician; if the person is hospitalized, the document should be put in the hospital record. Figure 7–1 contains a sample advance directive.

The advance directive gives every individual the right to determine medical treatment in dire situations, even when he or she can no longer directly make or communicate those wishes. It makes clear what the patient's wishes were when he or she was competent to designate them. Having a document saves the family members and medical staff the anguish of making these decisions without thorough knowledge of the patient's wishes. It circumvents differences of opinion among surviving relatives. It prevents a situation where the physician or medical staff makes no decision because of legal prohibitions, makes decisions that are discordant with the patient's wishes, or pursues a court-ordered medical decision to resolve the issue.

Planning and making goals for the future incorporates many spheres of activity in the life of the middle-aged and older person. Participating in all of these empowers each person to live fully and with as much a sense of mastery, determination, and dignity as possible.

FIGURE 7–1
Sample Advance Directive

D.C., Maryland and Virginia
ADVANCE DIRECTIVE

My Durable Power of Attorney for Health Care, Living Will and Other Wishes

I, _____, write this document as a directive regarding my medical care.

<u>Put the initials of your name by the choices you want.</u>

PART 1. MY DURABLE POWER OF ATTORNEY FOR HEALTH CARE.

_____ I appoint this person to make decisions about my medical care if there ever comes a time when I cannot make those decisions myself:

name	home phone	work phone

address

If the person above cannot or will not make decisions for me, I appoint this person:

name	home phone	work phone

address

_____ I have not appointed anyone to make health care decisions for me in this or any other document.

<u>I want the person I have appointed, my doctors, my family, and others to be guided by the decisions I have made below:</u>

Note: This is a sample document, prepared and distributed by the District of Columbia Hospital Association. Each jurisdiction will have its own requirements for language on such a document.

FIGURE 7–1 *Continued*

PART 2. MY LIVING WILL.

These are my wishes for my future medical care if there ever comes a time when I can't make these decisions for myself.

A. These are my wishes if I have a <u>terminal condition</u>:

Life-Sustaining Treatments

_____ I do not want life-sustaining treatments (including CPR) started. If life-sustaining treatments are started, I want them stopped.

_____ I want life-sustaining treatments that my doctors think are best for me.

_____ Other wishes: _____

Artificial Nutrition and Hydration

_____ I do not want artificial nutrition and hydration started if it would be the main treatment keeping me alive. If artificial nutrition and hydration is started, I want it stopped.

_____ I want artificial nutrition and hydration even if it is the main treatment keeping me alive.

_____ Other wishes: _____

Comfort Care

_____ I want to be kept as comfortable and free of pain as possible, even if such care prolongs my dying or shortens my life.

_____ Other wishes: _____

B. These are my wishes if I am ever in a <u>persistent vegetative state</u>:

Life-Sustaining Treatments

_____ I do not want life-sustaining treatments (including CPR) started. If life-sustaining treatments are started, I want them stopped.

_____ I want life-sustaining treatments that my doctors think are best for me.

_____ Other wishes: _____

Artificial Nutrition and Hydration

____ I do not want artificial nutrition and hydration started if it would be the main treatment keeping me alive. If artificial nutrition and hydration is started, I want it stopped.

____ I want artificial nutrition and hydration even if is the main treatment keeping me alive.

____ Other wishes:_____

Comfort Care

____ I want to be kept as comfortable and free of pain as possible, even if such care prolongs my dying or shortens my life.

____ Other wishes: _____

C.   Other Directions

You have the right to be involved in all decisions about your medical care, even those not dealing with terminal conditions or persistent vegetative states. If you have wishes not covered in other parts of this document, please indicate them here.

_____
_____
_____

PART 3. OTHER WISHES.

A.   Organ Donation

____ I do not wish to donate any of my organs or tissues.

____ I want to donate all of my organs and tissues.

____ I only want to donate these organs and tissues:

_____

____ Other wishes:_____

FIGURE 7–1 *Continued*

B. **Autopsy**

____ I do not want an autopsy.

____ I agree to an autopsy if my doctors wish it.

____ Other wishes: _____

If you wish to say more about any of the above choices, or if you have any other statements to make about your medical care, you may do so on a separate sheet of paper. If you do so, put here the number of pages you are adding: _____

PART 4. SIGNATURES.

You and two witnesses must sign this document in order for it to be legal.

A. **Your Signature.**

By my signature below I show that I understand the purpose and the effect of this document.

Signature:_____ Date: _____
Address: _____

B. **Your Witnesses' Signature**

I believe the person who has signed this advance directive to be of sound mind, that he/she signed or acknowledged this advance directive in my presence, and that he/she appears not to be acting under pressure, duress, fraud, or undue influence. I am not related to the person making this advance directive by blood, marriage or adoption, nor, to the best of my knowledge, am I named in his/her will. I am not the person appointed in this advance directive. I am not a health care provider or an employee of health care provider who is now, or has been in the past, responsible for the care of the person making this advance directive.

Witness #1

Signature:_____ Date: _____
Address: _____

Witness #2

Signature:_____ Date: _____
Address: _____

Words You Need to Know:

Advance Directive: A written document that tells what a person wants or does not want if he/she in the future can't make his/her wishes known about medical treatment.

Artificial Nutrition and Hydration: When food and water are fed to a person through a tube.

Autopsy: An examination done on a dead body to find the cause of death.

Comfort Care: Care that helps to keep a person comfortable but does not make him/her better. Bathing, turning, keeping a person's lips moist are types of comfort care.

CPR (Cardiopulmonary Resuscitation): Treatment to try and restart a person's breathing or heartbeat. CPR may be done by pushing on the chest, by putting a tube down the throat, or by other treatment.

Durable Power of Attorney for Health Care: An advance directive that appoints someone to make medical decisions for a person if in the future he/she can't make his/her own medical decisions.

Life-Sustaining Treatment: Any medical treatment that is used to keep a person from dying. A breathing machine, CPR, and artificial nutrition and hydration are examples of life-sustaining treatments.

Living Will: An advance directive that tells what medical treatment a person does or does not want if he/she is not able to make his/her wishes known.

Organ and Tissue Donation: When a person permits his/her organs (such as eyes or kidneys) and other parts of the body (such as skin) to be removed after death to be transplanted for use by another person or to be used for experimental purposes.

Persistent Vegetative State: When a person is unconscious with no hope of regaining consciousness even with medical treatment. The body may move and eyes may be open but as far as anyone can tell, the person can't think or respond.

Terminal Condition: An on-going condition caused by injury or illness that has no cure and from which doctors expect the person to die even with medical treatment. Life-sustaining treatments will only prolong a person's dying if the person is suffering from a terminal condition.

PART II

Psychological Problems in the Later Years

8

When Is a Problem a Problem?

The previous chapters have described psychological or developmental issues that many people experience in later life. They include expectations, challenges, and changes that older people encounter, and they involve struggles, which, although distressing at times, can be dealt with by using coping skills and the supportive resources of family, friends, or others in the community. The appreciation of one's lifelines of relationships, experiences, and inherent capabilities provides basic personal assets, which can and should be mobilized in these efforts. An attitude of hope and optimism gives an added boost as older adults work to use their later years for maximum functioning and happiness, in spite of inevitable deterioration.

Growing older is stressful at any age. At each stage of life there are developmental tasks, conflicts, pains, and joys. Growing older, whether from 10 to 20 or from 70 to 80, brings a complex mixture of feelings, thoughts, stresses, and successes. Aging brings with it change in all kinds of ways: with old and new relationships, experiences, ways of coping, hardships, and gratifications. We try to adapt to new demands and cope with new or repeated stresses. At every age, the experience of growing older seems problematic at the time. The middle and later years, however, bring the added complications of deteriorative physical changes, life-threatening illnesses, and death in the not-too-distant future. Living and aging successfully involves confronting these complications and attempting to master the more difficult elements while relishing the others.

The term *over the hill* has been used for various milestones in the aging process. It conveys the notion of being less useful or even useless, of falling out of sight. It is as if the person who has reached 65, or 70, and certainly 80, has fallen off a cliff. In fact, there is no real phenomenon of falling off a cliff, at any age. No one should automatically accept the idea of getting old or being "over the hill" as an excuse for significant physical or emotional changes in the middle and later years. Those who do are accepting disability, which is more than the usually slow changes that accompany normal aging. In any one period of six months or a year, no adult will change very drastically in any respect because of aging. If there are dramatic changes in behavior, thinking ability, stamina, mood, or memory in a short time span, there are reasons, medical or psychological, beyond "just getting old," and those reasons should be identified by consulting appropriate professionals. Any changes that result in significant diminution of physical or emotional function need to be addressed. The distinctions between what is the product of normal aging in the later years and what is not are sometimes blurry, but it is vital that those distinctions be clarified. It is therefore pertinent to ask, "When is a problem a problem?"

A problem is a problem when life is significantly different than it recently has been or when the ability to function in one or more aspects of life is noticeably diminished in a short period of time. Without being overly preoccupied with the problems of life, it is worth taking stock, periodically, of one's state of health, physical and mental, and asking, Am I doing all right? How am I compared to six months or a year ago? Are there things I did just a short time ago that I'm not doing or I'm no longer able to do? Are there new things I want to do that I'm not pursuing? Sometimes these questions are hard to answer. We may forget how things were just a short time ago, and the assistance of friends, family, or physician may be necessary to arrive at some answers. Sometimes family members and friends notice first that something is not quite right. There are some issues that promote or exaggerate problems in living and others that must be evaluated to determine whether a problem exists.

Underestimating Strengths

More than at any other time of life, it is vital that older adults not doubt or underestimate their strengths and coping skills. Many do so, even though they admit to being quite competent just several years or even months earlier. Some people are too ready to see themselves as significantly impaired merely because of advanced age (although the particular age chosen varies with each individual). In those situations, problems more quickly become problems. A dramatic example concerns a 77-year-old woman who consulted me for an evaluation of the recent onset of anxiety.

Mrs. P. saw herself as moderately impaired by anxiety and dizziness. In her third session with me, there was an extremely violent thunderstorm, and rain, hail, and wind pelted the large window in my office. We continued to work at understanding some of her concerns while remarking on the unusually powerful storm. I left my office shortly after she did and was amazed by the devastation caused by the storm. Large trees had been uprooted and had fallen across parked automobiles and houses. Electric power and telephone lines were down. Traffic was at a standstill. I wondered what happened to the elderly woman who had left my office fifteen minutes earlier and briefly looked for her before abandoning my own car and walking home. Several days later I reached her by telephone. After our session, she had gone out to the street and found that a large tree had fallen on her car, smashing all four side windows but leaving the windshield and rear window intact. She asked three young men to help her lift the tree from the car and to clear some tree limbs in her path to a major thoroughfare, which was passable. With their assistance, she drove home and later arranged to have her car repaired.

This woman thought of herself as formerly rather robust but more recently quite fragile, yet she was able to mobilize strengths that she no longer thought were available. She had begun to think of herself as rather invalided by her physical and psychological symptoms. Although she still required treatment, the unusual event of the freak storm and its consequences reawakened in her a sense of hopefulness that she had considerable competence. Maybe she possessed some old, and continuing, strengths that were available to her for everyday life as well, and maybe some of her problems were not really problems.

Most people do not experience such dramatic tests of their coping abilities, but throughout life we assess and test our strengths and weaknesses in our minds and in our actions. The later years require that we realize, consider, and maximize our many strengths to attempt to diminish ongoing problems and occasional crises.

Ignoring a Problem

One of the common ways in which older people deal with problems, particularly psychological ones but also physical ones, is to attribute them to normal aging. While some amount of denial is adaptive and even protective of the individual, in excess it can be dangerous because the problem is never faced, and the victim may live, unnecessarily, as an untreated invalid, or even worse, may precipitate premature death. An example involves a man who attempted to ignore an insidious and potentially dangerous problem, ascribing depressive signs and symptoms to the proclivities of aging.

> Mr. A., a 75-year-old vigorous widowed man, began spending more and more of his day in bed. He had adjusted well to his widowhood of five years, but recently he felt that life was "hardly worth living." He said that he just wanted to be alone. He could not account for this change in his outlook; his health continued to be good, and he had suffered no recent reverses, he thought. His physician of many years found no evidence of illness on physical examination and attributed his change in mood and activity to "old age" but said, none-

theless, that he might benefit from "talking with someone." At his alarmed daughter's insistence, Mr. A. consulted a psychiatrist, who felt that his problem was one of mild to moderate depression precipitated by the recent deaths of several of Mr. A.'s walking partners and complicated by a recent increase in his alcohol consumption, which he had thought would make him feel better. Although Mr. A. was in no acute danger at this point, the depression and increased alcohol intake might have led to decreased appetite, weight loss, weakness, dehydration, and many other problems, including a spiral of deepening depression. He was even at risk for possible suicide.

The psychiatrist scheduled several sessions with Mr. A. in which they discussed his losses and his many strengths. Mr. A. felt he had "lived long enough" and had had a good life. He agreed that he had recently ignored the positive aspects of his life and had "fallen into bad patterns" since the deaths of his friends. He felt better after the several sessions, and he wanted to see if he could manage his life better. With the help of a community organization, Mr. A. began to attend Alcoholics Anonymous meetings and joined an ongoing exercise group composed of people of ages 50 to 75 years. He said that he would again consult with a psychiatrist if he "couldn't lick it" himself. Mr. A. had a problem, the magnitude of which he chose largely to deny. If not labeled, assessed, and dealt with, it may have led to more serious consequences.

Depression in later life is a serious medical-psychiatric illness, which many people, like Mr. A., would ascribe to aging and/or to deny its impact and consequences. Depression, with profound sadness, feelings of hopelessness, lack of pleasure in one's usual activities, and other associated symptoms, is always a problem and should be vigorously pursued. The distinction between normal grief and depression is sometimes blurry. We certainly do best if we experience bereavement according to our personal styles and not label it as a disorder. Even if we are quite liberal in the definition of grief, however, the symptoms of a complicated bereavement can sometimes become so extreme that some professional intervention is required. That is a serious but treatable problem to be faced.

The same issues arise in the denial of medical problems. Undiagnosed pain, bleeding, swelling, fever, changes in bowel and urinary functions, difficulty breathing, changes in weight, increased fatigue, and other new symptoms are usually the result of medical problems that may not be particularly serious but may be debilitating or at least bothersome. Sometimes they represent the early signs of a serious problem, which, if brought to the attention of a physician, may be diagnosed and treated successfully. Aging often serves as an excuse offered for these, but it is rarely the cause of any of the symptoms mentioned. Some older (and younger) people deny or ignore symptoms because they worry about some catastrophic diagnosis, or even death, and, irrationally, they would rather not hear the bad news. Others think they "know" that their symptoms are significant and pessimistically prejudge their prognosis saying, "Nothing can be done anyway, so why bother getting treatment." Still others are depressed and immobilized; they do not have the energy or inclination to get help with what might be an easily diagnosed and treatable problem. For the vital older adult, the threat of an illness can be a major crisis, and for the chronically ill person, it represents continued and increased frustration and disability. The reaction to any illness, and the extent to which denial is used excessively and maladaptively, is very much determined by personality characteristics, the personal history of the individual, recent and past health history, and family experiences with illness.

Most medical problems are not serious or life threatening. For those that are potentially serious, early diagnosis offers the best hope for successful treatment for symptomatic relief and cure. Family members and friends should exert considerable pressure on older adults who tend to deny physical and psychological symptoms, so that maximal functioning is pursued by evaluating signs and symptoms and treating any diagnosed disorders.

Forgetting

One of the most worrisome and common gray areas older people confront is that of forgetting. As people age, they continue to remember early experiences fairly well but increasingly forget common words or things that they should know, even the names of people they know well are not immediately available for recall. They forget one of the three chores that need to be done, and without a list, shopping for more than four items is an impossible task. It is true that starting even in the late 20s and early 30s, recall of names and words is slowed and increasingly difficult. If we add in the effects of anxiety or preoccupation with failing memory and other stresses, the memory difficulties are considerably exaggerated. Usually, with some techniques for retrieval, people can remember what they need, albeit after several minutes of going through the alphabet or associating to related items or by just relaxing. This kind of forgetting is usually not an indication of early dementia; it is a part of normal aging. If the difficulty increases over a short time or if the forgetting begins to significantly affect social relationships, work, or usual activities over a period of months, a physician should be consulted to evaluate the nature of the problem. (See also chapter 10.)

Anxiety Disorders

Although the common psychiatric problems of depression and dementia are described in detail in the next two chapters, there are other emotional problems which affect older adults. Anxiety disorders—generalized anxiety, panic disorders, phobias, obsessive-compulsive disorders, and posttraumatic stress disorders—occur in older people. There are some variations in symptoms with each of the specific disorders, but they have in common subjective feelings of nervousness, apprehension, and uneasiness. In addition, patients may experience palpitations, distress in breathing, and sweating. Anxiety is a major component of depression in older people. It is associated with dementia and alcohol abuse and may be coincident with some medical disorders (hyperthyroidism, heart disease) and as adverse effects of various medications. Older adults who have suffered traumatic events as survivors of war, forcible confinement, or victims of crimes may demonstrate posttraumatic anxiety, both immediately and months and years after the event.

Anxiety disorders are disabling medical-psychiatric conditions with which older people often suffer quietly, attempting to reorganize their life-styles to cope with the resulting handicaps. Anxious older adults, whether phobic or concerned about panic attacks, may remain as prisoners in their apartments for months or years rather than venture outside, where they feel vulnerable to incapacitating symptoms. The repercussions of these behaviors can extend to poor nutrition because shopping for food is not regularly done, failure to seek medical attention because it usually means going to a clinic or physician's office, and lack of exercise, entertainment, and socialization as their world becomes more and more confined.

After proper diagnosis, anxiety disorders are treatable, and those afflicted usually have increased freedom to function to their potential when the symptoms are alleviated. The primary treatments of anxiety are psychotherapy and medications. Benzodiazepines and some newer antianxiety (anxiolytic) medications are prescribed for generalized anxiety and panic disorder. The latter may also be treated with some antidepressants. Other kinds of antidepressant medications, particularly the newer serotonin-enhancing agents, are used for obsessive-compulsive disorders and combinations of psychotherapy and benzodiazepines for phobic symptoms. (See also chapter 9.) Anxiety disorders are real problems that must be presented to physicians and other mental health professionals, just as are other medical conditions, so that life patterns are not dictated by the invalidism they can cause.

The next chapters describe two psychiatric difficulties common in the later years. They are clearly major problems and should not be dismissed as or ascribed to normal aging. Although these disorders are different in many respects, both require diligence to diagnose and treat to the extent possible, so that the later years can be ones of maximum function. Depression, most often undiagnosed or misdiagnosed, has a very high rate of successful treatment. Dementia remains a great challenge, in both diagnosis and treatment. Nonetheless, although the cognitive deficits cannot yet be reversed, many people who suffer with dementia can be helped to use existing function maximally and to benefit from treatment of related symptoms.

In considering these problems, it is crucial to recognize that everyone has a personal history of relationships, experiences, inherent capabilities, and personality characteristics that yield strengths, weaknesses, and coping skills. All of these interact, in a complex way, with inborn biological factors, which we are only beginning to understand. Problems are problems when the sum of these produces impaired functioning and disability.

9

Depression:
A Treatable Disorder

"To be old and sad is double jeopardy," said an 85-year-old man who was increasingly aware of the disability caused by his depression. Indeed it is. Depression is more than sadness. It is a state of sadness that does not seem to go away and is accompanied by feelings of hopelessness, worthlessness, and helplessness, withdrawal from activities of daily life, changes in appetite and sleep patterns, and maybe even difficulty thinking straight. Sometimes people feel that it would be all right if they were "just hit by a truck," and others have more active suicidal thoughts. Depression of varying severity affects approximately 15 percent of the older population. Whatever its symptoms, it can be treated successfully more than 75 percent of the time. Depression is a problem that is most often accepted by the general public, physicians, and others as "just a part of getting older." Depression is *not* a part of normal aging; it is a medical disorder, and like hypertension or diabetes, it can and must be treated when it interferes with otherwise healthy functioning.

Mrs. B. is a 75-year-old woman who had been widowed for more than a decade. Over the last year, after the death of a close friend, she became depressed, feeling that nothing was fun anymore. She had had an active social life, participated in several organizations, and enjoyed visiting her two children and three grandchildren. In the last year, all of these seemed less important than they had been. She was not been sleeping well, her appetite had decreased, and she had lost ten pounds. She had begun to avoid friends and activities, feeling that she was "too sad" to be with people. Mrs. B. felt that this was no way to live; she wanted to find out what was wrong with her and, if possible, get some help. She was evaluated medically and psychologically and was thought to be moderately depressed. The death of her close friend, a major loss for her in its own right, had also reactivated an accumulation of feelings related to the deaths of other significant people in her life. After brief treatment with psychotherapy and medications, Mrs. B. felt "back to normal."

Mrs. B's story again raises the question of what is normal in the later years and what is not. After some significant losses of spouse, children, and friends, there is, of course, expectable sadness and mourning. Mrs. B. had a feeling that this was more than that; she had experienced other important losses and had not reacted with so much disability. Sometimes because of the extent of the symptoms and loss of function, it is obvious that one is suffering with depression. Sometimes those affected with depression do not have the energy, judgment, or insight to seek treatment, and that job falls to family, friends, professionals, and others with whom the older person interacts. Often the distinction between mourning and a depressive disorder is a subtle one that can be made only by a careful history and observation over a period of time.

Vulnerabilities

Although most older adults are generally healthy, aging leaves everyone subject to vulnerabilities that they may not have encountered in earlier years. Some of these may predispose to depression.

Reserve Capacity

One significant vulnerability of the later years is a seeming lack of reserve capacity. It is true that most older adults are generally healthy, but they may not have the reserve or flexibility to cope with multiple stresses, medical or psychological. They may operate within a narrower band of function than do younger people, and deviations from the narrow range may bring symptoms that produce a decrease in functioning.

A 20-year-old college student, afflicted with a viral pneumonia, feels sick, is coughing, has a fever and chills, wants someone to take care of him, and worries about when he can get back to classes, play basketball, and resume his social life. In a week or two, he is mostly back to normal. His 80-year-old grandmother, who becomes ill with the same virus, may have a more complicated course. Because of her brittleness, her coughing causes a rib to fracture. She may easily become dehydrated because, with the fever, she did not feel like drinking fluids. She may then become somewhat delirious, lose track of time, not move much out of bed, and possibly develop a secondary bacterial infection. She may become unsteady as she attempts to go to the bathroom at night and fall, possibly bruising her knee or fracturing her hip. She feels so debilitated. She thinks that this is no way to live and she becomes increasingly depressed. In this case, the grandmother's medical problems progress because of the lack of reserve or flexibility to cope with the initial physical assault of a severe viral infection and the consequent spiral of deterioration.

Similarly, in terms of primarily psychological issues, people may become less able to deal with stress as they age. They tend to become less flexible in schedules, activities, meal times, diets, and general patterns. As they feel out of control of so many aspects of life, adults may seek to control the aspects that they can, in turn making them less tolerant of the inevitable surprises, crises, and changes of the later years. In addition, some of the adaptive coping skills of the past may be less available. Hard work, athletics, and other physical outlets may have to be adjusted for age. Changes in hearing, vision, taste, and stamina may add to a generalized feeling that coping reserve or flexibility is decreased. Some of these are partially offset by the positive value of personality characteristics and strengths that have been practiced over many years. None of these changes implies that one is ill; rather, they mean that some parts are wearing and one has to learn how to cope with the vulnerability they may bring.

Family members and friends who recognize the fragility of otherwise healthy older people close to them can play an important role in buoying up their elders who feel unduly taxed. Family may be able to lend some support and coping skills to help an older person get through a difficult situation or phase, so that despair and depression can be warded off.

A 65-year-old woman, Mrs. E., moved across the country to be closer to her son, daughter-in-law, and grandchildren. She had planned to work in retail sales, but on arrival in her new city, she found no available work opportunities. She became despairing of ever finding work and became withdrawn and sad. She lumped all her anxiety about the move into her lack of work. A granddaughter who had volunteered in a hospital recognized Mrs. E.'s distress and spent several afternoons accompanying her on visits to community centers to investigate recreational possibilities and to department stores to seek work. Not only did those afternoons prove to be very fruitful in terms of employment, but Mrs. E. came away feeling well supported in her new venture, and her granddaughter learned much about her grandmother from the intimate time together.

Biological Changes

A number of studies demonstrate that there are significant changes in the amount and nature of the brain chemicals (neurotransmitters) as aging proceeds. There are also changes in the receptors in the brain that are affected by those neurotransmitters. The relative decreases in some neurotransmitters, increases in others, and changes in receptors may have roles in predisposing some older adults to depression. Hormones from the thyroid, adrenal, and pituitary glands may change in quantity and quality with aging and allow for a greater susceptibility to depression. Although there is a loss of neurons in the brain, both randomly and in certain defined areas of the brain, it is unclear how much these changes predispose to depression.

The acuteness of sensory functions, particularly vision, hearing, taste, and smell, diminishes with aging and predisposes to decreased contact with people and the environment. Social interactions are more difficult, and activities such as reading, listening to the radio, watching television, and others that require or are enhanced by good sensory functioning are less enjoyable or even impossible. Changes in hair, skin, muscle tone, stamina, and vigor are daily physical reminders of the aging process and its biological consequences, which contribute to a feeling of vulnerability.

Losses

Inherent in the aging process is the reality of loss—loss of stamina, some sensory functions, flexibility, status, financial stability, health, and, probably of most importance, loved ones and friends. Losses are inevitable; they are a part of everyone's life experience. They are a greater challenge to coping skills than any other emotional experiences. Over time, the losses become cumulative and more intense. Most people deal with their losses successfully; others find them overwhelming, bringing a sense of loneliness and despair.

It is not only the current losses that can predispose people to depression but also the reliving of losses sustained earlier in life, which were not satisfactorily worked through, mourned, or otherwise resolved. Sometimes the most mourned losses leave a scar that never fully recedes and may resurface on anniversaries, birthdays, and with other reminders.

A 55-year-old woman whose mother had died of cancer when she was 9 years old became tearful whenever she heard about someone with cancer. She did not feel sad on a daily basis about her mother's death, but hearing about a similar illness of others evoked a brief spontaneous and uncontrollable emotional response of tearing and a feeling of "a lump in the throat." She said, "At age 9 I wasn't ready to lose my mother." The consistency of her reaction, well into adulthood, made her aware of the impact of that loss.

Retirement

Retirement, for many, offers the prospect of some golden years after many years of work. It offers opportunities for time that is relatively free from the responsibility of children, time for extended vacations not taken earlier, time to try a new career, avocation, or learn new skills, and time to spend with spouse, friends, adult children, and grandchildren. Retirement works this way for many people, particularly those who are relatively healthy, have reasonable financial resources, and have planned to some extent how they would spend those years.

For other people, retirement is not so golden. It may be another reminder of loss—of job, career, status, "the place to hang your hat," a place to socialize. Retirement may provoke marital tensions that may be new or uncovered as a result of the stresses inherent in retirement. Sometimes retirement involves a move away from a familiar neighborhood or part of the country. Retirement stresses can make one more vulnerable to depression.

Medical Problems

Medical illness is not pleasant to endure at any age, and for older adults, it is even more arduous. Although most older adults are generally healthy, the prevalence of chronic illness is great. Arthritis, heart disease, hypertension, diabetes, cancer, osteoporosis, losses of hearing and vision, and strokes are among the more common afflictions of older people. Older people who already feel strained by the normal aspects of aging meet the increased disability of a cold, flu, pneumonia, and more severe illnesses with worry, discouragement, and, at times, fears of permanent invalidism and death. Beside the actual consequences of a medical illness, even a rather minor illness in the later years is a signal for some people that life has taken a major turn for the worse. We often hear an elderly person predicting, "I'll never leave the hospital alive," when there is no justification for gloom. The patient may see an illness as further depriving him or her of diminishing control over life. Most illnesses, even in older adults, are not life-threatening, however, and they usually respond to treatment and recover. The recuperation may be lengthier than it is in younger adults, and the possibilities of complications are more real.

Older adults, like people at all other ages, have varying styles in the ways they cope with medical illness. Some deny or minimize their problems, wanting to go on with their lives and not fully focus on the medical problem. At the other extreme are those who overly dramatize or exaggerate their physical signs and symptoms. Either pattern may be the product of personality traits and coping styles and secondary anxiety and depression.

Hip fractures and surgical procedures are well tolerated by most people, even the oldest old, but they may be the focal points for onset of depression, particularly if there are complications or if recovery is slower than the patient anticipates. They may be a reminder of older relatives or friends who "died on the table" in a previous era when surgery was more dangerous to older adults. Physicians and other professionals who work with the elderly should be alert to the possibility of these reactions. They can attempt to prevent them with adequate preparation of the patient for surgery, including caring support and accurate information about the procedure, immediate postoperative pain and disability, and longer-term recuperation. They can actively treat or seek consultation for any psychological complications when they occur.

More than 50 percent of those who sustain strokes may become depressed in the two years after those catastrophic events. The onset of depression after a stroke is likely to be caused by the specific organic damage to nerve pathways in the brain that produce certain neurotransmitter chemicals, as well as to the psychological trauma that ensues. Research studies and clinical experience have demonstrated that depression due to these causes can be treated successfully, using antidepressant medications alone or in combination with psychotherapy.

Medications

Advances in the development of medications since the early 1970s have revolutionized the treatment of general medical and psychiatric illnesses. Medications, old and new, have an important role in the lives of older adults. More than a third of the medications prescribed by physicians are consumed by people over the age of 65—about 13 percent of the general population. I have known people to take as many as sixteen different medicines, dispensed in up to forty-two pills per day—quite a task.

For many people, medications are life saving; others permit older adults to function at their best in spite of acute or chronic illness. We are increasingly coming to understand, however, that some medications, alone or in combination with others (and sometimes many others), can produce unpleasant and sometimes dangerous side effects. Depression, other changes in mental status, and changes in thinking ability are possible adverse effects to which older people are susceptible. Almost any medication can produce these dangerous effects, but the most commonly implicated are the antihypertensives, cardiac antiarrhythmics, anti-inflammatory, and beta-blocking agents. This does not mean that anyone taking one or more of these medications will become depressed or should stop taking the drugs if side effects develop. Rather, physicians and patients need to be alert and in communication about the fact that any medication *might* be causing mental changes, such as depression or cognitive impairment, and thoroughly investigate to find the cause. At least several medications are available to treat any one medical condition, and an alternative can sometimes be given after consultation with the primary care physician. Sometimes a physician will advise lowering the dose of a drug to eliminate or lessen the troublesome side effects.

Mental changes as adverse effects of a medication may occur soon after a drug is prescribed or after many years of successful use. As people age, there are changes in the ways medications are absorbed, metabolized, and eliminated, and it is impossible to predict when a significant change will affect a prescribed medication. Geriatricians have noted that medications that were legitimately prescribed for a patient's medical problem in the past may no longer be required later. Individual idiosyncratic biological reactions obviously play a role in this matter. All of these issues must be taken into account in any medical regimen, and medications (prescribed, over the counter, and borrowed from relatives and friends) consumed must be regularly reviewed for their possible side effects and their continued efficacy and necessity. When dealing with an older adult, a physician often does more good by taking away a medication than by adding a new one.

Thoughts of Death

A typical healthy 19-year-old thinks of himself as invulnerable or close to it, and only in extraordinary circumstances would thoughts of his death enter his mind. As one ages, with each successive decade, it is obvious to most people that they are closer to death than they ever have been. In the later years, we are frequently aware, in a more poignant way than ever before, that death is a probability in the not-too-distant future. People deal with this awareness in a variety of ways, depending on their individual histories and personality styles, but it is most uncommon, at least in the current generation of elderly, to talk about the subject very much, except when one is depressed or otherwise ill.

There is an axiom in psychiatry that some denial of the facts of life (and death) may be psychically, and even physically, protective. A man who has just sustained a heart attack may deny the extent of the damage done to his heart muscle and the ways it will change his life. Nonetheless, he follows the directions of his physician with regard to his care. His denial mechanism does not interfere with his care and may be important to his future functioning; the denial should be left undisturbed. At other times, a person, young or old, is preoccupied with an upsetting thought—death is a common one—and would welcome the simple acknowledgment of that thought. Some people might be ready for broader discussions of their thoughts, feelings, or fears about death; having someone available to listen could be a great relief. It is a difficult subject to confront. Unfortunately, few of us can tolerate that kind of involvement and intimacy. I do not encourage or discourage family, friends, or professionals from discussing these issues but rather emphasize that unexpressed concerns about death can become preoccupying for some older people and may be another source of vulnerability to depression. Talking about death does not have to be taboo.

Recurrent Depression

Although I have emphasized some vulnerabilities to depression that are specific to later life, there is a significant group of people who have been depressed for many years, maybe for most of their lives, with periodic recurrences, which tend to increase in frequency with increasing age. There are frequently genetic and other biological underpinnings to these situations; often there is a history of other family members with depression. The stresses of the later years are relevant and may be responsible for a specific depressive episode.

Obviously there is a complex network of factors than can conspire to produce or precipitate depression in an older person. Fortunately, they rarely all converge. Nowhere else is the interweaving of biological, sociocultural, medical, and psychological issues so apparent. Vulnerability and susceptibility are important to acknowledge, to watch for, and to assist with when possible. They do not imply a chronic mental illness or doom. Depression is not a part of normal aging; rather, it is a treatable illness that expresses itself with signs and symptoms, to which we must be attentive.

Signs and Symptoms of Depression

"I have no energy, my bowels don't work, and my head aches all the time; I don't enjoy anything anymore; I'm old; I don't know what you mean by 'depressed.'"

Blaming an invalided state on aging, the older person may accept the notion that this is all part of the aging process, or he or she may not really know what *depression* means. For many people in the current generation of elderly, *depression* means that you are lazy, crazy, or making excuses for yourself. It may represent something that you should "just snap out of," and if you do not, you have something morally or characterologically wrong with you. Because of these misconceptions, the signs and symptoms of depression are often ignored until they become incapacitating or until someone else recognizes them.

The signs and symptoms of depression are the clues that help clinicians make a diagnosis of depression. The signs are the objective indications of a problem that are observable by other people in the environment: walking slowly and hunched over, not smiling much, and looking unkempt. The symptoms are the subjective changes or complaints that are felt or reported by the patient: sadness, "lump in the throat," feelings of hopelessness. The signs and symptoms are what the clinician—family physician, psychiatrist, or other professional—will be assessing in an effort to define and diagnose the problem. An older depressed person may have some signs and symptoms that are common across the age spectrum and others that are peculiar to the elderly. Clinicians often have to persevere in their efforts to discover the range of signs and symptoms that might point to depression in a given patient, in the face of frequent denials, misconceptions, and obfuscations.

Signs

What does the depressed person look like? An array of signs may be apparent in various combinations over a period of time. Sometimes the best observers are those who see the person only occasionally; when you spend time with someone on a daily basis, you may miss the gradual changes in appearance that may occur. A relative or friend visiting after weeks or months of absence might say, "Dad really looks terrible; he's not himself. He looks as though he's aged a lot in the last three months. Is he ill?" Depressed people may look unkempt; they may not take care of their hair, teeth, and skin as they had previously. They may "forget" to bathe or to change or wash their clothes. They may say, when questioned, that they do not care how they look, or "I just don't have the energy anymore," or they may be oblivious to their inattention to toileting and self-care. One wife of a depressed man complained that her husband had "a drawer full of shirts," but he insisted on wearing the same worn-out flannel shirt every day and he did not care whether it was laundered. In years past, he had been quite fastidious about his clothes. This change was one of the early signs of depression. Comparisons with behavior and personality characteristics prior to the onset of signs of a problem are crucial.

Depressed people look sad, although they do not necessarily voice a complaint of sadness. They may be teary-eyed or cry for no apparent reason or after recalling sad events of the past. They might feel very sad but may not be able to cry. They may openly speak of suicide or say that it would be just as well if they did not wake up in the morning. They may withdraw from activities or just go through the motions. Even major family occasions, such as birthdays, weddings, and holidays, seem not to be enjoyed as they had in the past.

Depressed people seem slowed down. They may look as though they can barely walk from one place to another, as if their feet were extremely heavy. Speech may be slowed, even distorted, like a record playing at the wrong speed. They may not speak as much as they had in the past or not at all. They may appear tired all the time but complain that they cannot sleep. At the other extreme, older people who are depressed may be jittery, agitated, anxious, or almost hyperactive, unable to sit in one place and relax. They may pace from one room to the next or fidget with objects. They may start a project but not complete it. Family members may notice that a depressed relative is not eating, is losing weight, and looks as though he has a chronic illness.

Symptoms

Even if the older person does not complain about depression, he or she will frequently feel and complain about things that can add up to depression. These complaints generally fall into several common categories.

PHYSICAL COMPLAINTS. Physical symptoms are the most prominent complaints of the older person. Older people, justly or not, are known for their "aches and pains," and, indeed, as we age, we all have more physical distress. But depressed people may become preoccupied with their fatigue, abdominal distress, headaches, chest pains, and arthritis. Legitimate preexisting medical problems become exaggerated and may mask or disguise depression. Primary care physicians often become frustrated because they cannot seem to fit the extent of the complaints with an evident illness, or sometimes, with any illness, and they may write off the patients as chronic complainers when they do not get better. Some physicians see through the disguise and entertain the diagnosis of depression when physical complaints are abundant and no other medical diagnosis is apparent.

Other physical complaints that have diagnostic significance include the vegetative symptoms often described as the hallmarks of moderate to severe depression: loss of appetite and weight; sleep disturbances, usually characterized by early morning awakenings or multiple awakenings during the night, with difficulty falling back to sleep; constipation; and chronic fatigue.

Sleep disturbances must be carefully evaluated by the clinician. They are frequent complaints of older people in general, and of depressed people in particular. Although early morning awakenings or multiple nighttime awakenings are the most commonly experienced sleep disturbances, it is essential to compare these patterns with the patient's usual sleep pattern prior to the onset of depression. Sleep time may be occurring at various times of the day, so that total hours of sleep are not abnormal. Daytime napping is a common replacement for sleep at night. Sleep disturbances are so discomforting to the older person that they may seek to use, and perhaps abuse, alcohol and other medications, some of which are extremely dangerous for them. Abnormal sleep patterns should be carefully evaluated by a physician. Some patterns are indicative of medical disorders, including depression, and should be assessed so that proper behavioral or pharmacological treatment can be prescribed.

Sexual activity is important to most older adults. Depression often disrupts the usual sexual desires, interest, and functioning of an individual or couple. Rarely, sexual activity is increased, and the spouse or mate senses that the other is especially clingy and dependent, wanting to be held and touched a great deal. Failure in sexual activity can be a most distressing symptom for the older person who previously enjoyed sex and is a complaint that rarely is addressed. The older patient may not necessarily relate the sexual disturbance with depression but see it as further evidence of deterioration due to aging and feel that he or she must learn how to endure it. Some patients see their sexual difficulties as evidence of the harm they are doing to their mates and feel guilty that they cannot perform better.

Increased use and abuse of alcohol and other drugs may be a symptom of depression. Although there are many reasons that alcohol and other substances are abused, one that is sometimes not considered is the conscious or unconscious desperate attempt to self-medicate a depressive disorder. Alcohol and most other substances abused by the elderly are powerful depressants, and their use greatly complicates both the psychiatric and general medical states of the patient. Alcohol has profound effects on the brain, liver, kidneys, and cardiovascular systems, and its abuse often results in inadequate diet, malnutrition, poor hygiene, and more general deterioration. Alcohol abusers, no matter what their age, often deny the significance and amount of their alcohol intake. Friends and family members should regard alcohol abuse as a possibly serious symptom of depression or other psychiatric problem.

EMOTIONAL SYMPTOMS. Older people who are depressed do not feel well; some may say they are sad or blue or just "not right." Many deny their sadness and depression; those who are more seriously affected have trouble hiding their feelings of hopelessness, helplessness, and worthlessness, which are among the core emotional symptoms of depression at any age. They intrude on the life they knew prior to the onset of depression.

- A grandmother doesn't want her grandchildren to visit: "I used to be a good cookie baker, but nothing is right now; I don't even remember how to use the oven."
- A lawyer, reknowned in his specialty, does not want to take new cases. He says, "I'm a fraud; my partners are probably looking for ways to let me go."
- The construction foreman does not have the energy to get to the job. With resignation he says, "It's over; I'll never be the same."

Excessive worries about finances, family, health, responsibilities, and past deeds and misdeeds become exaggerated in depression. They may have some basis in reality, but with depression these issues becomes themes on which to ruminate. Again, it is essential to see the older person in the context of his or her personal history. How has he or she changed, and since when have the ups and downs of daily life become preoccupying or almost paralyzing worries?

Crying, tearing up, or feeling on the verge of tears can be perplexing, embarrassing, and distressing to the older person. Feelings of emptiness, demoralization, and uselessness are felt in depression and sometimes are linked to suicidal thoughts. "I should be thrown in the garbage," one man said. These feelings can take the extreme form of a delusion—a fixed false belief that cannot be verified in reality. We hear people say that their "guts are rotting; I have a cancer growing in my stomach; there are maggots in my stomach." Sometimes they express the emptiness with feelings of "being a shell; having a hole somewhere inside [pointing to the head or abdomen]."

Although depressed people are usually withdrawn and passive, they may be irritable, disagreeable, and negativistic—finding fault with people and things that would otherwise be acceptable. A previously doting 69-year-old grandfather exploded at his grandson for dropping a box of nails on the floor of his workshop. He said that he was too old to have helpers and his grandson should learn from someone else. The irritability and overreaction were aspects of his depressive disorder.

THINKING (COGNITIVE) SYMPTOMS. People often do not associate thinking difficulties or distortions with depression. Young and old people have thinking disturbances that may be primarily due to depression. A depressed college student may find that she has difficulty concentrating while studying for a course; her thinking is slowed and less sharp while trying to understand the questions on an examination. An older person may not remember his address or telephone number or may think that someone is tapping his telephone. Thinking disturbances manifested by memory failure, difficulty concentrating, delusions (fixed false beliefs), and hallucinations (auditory, visual, or other sensory perceptions that are not based on reality or external stimuli) may be associated with severe depression as well as with other psychiatric and neurological conditions. When a clinician hears about or assesses these symptoms, it is important to distinguish which, among the possible diagnoses, may be causing them.

The term *pseudodementia*, now usually referred to as the *dementia of depression*, has been used to describe the dementia-like symptoms of memory loss, language difficulties, diminished concentration and learning capacity, and decrease in functioning in the routine activities of daily living that may accompany severe depression, particularly in older people. When dementia is a presenting symptom, it is sometimes difficult to determine whether it is due to an organic brain disorder, such as Alzheimer's disease, or to depression. Because there is still no confirmatory test for many of the dementias, including Alzheimer's disease, clinicians often go through an extensive battery of diagnostic tests to try to ascertain a correct diagnosis. Sometimes they may treat the patient with an antidepressant medication to see if the symptoms abate. Since up to half of the patients who have dementia also have a significant clinical depression, they too may benefit from a medication trial of this sort, although an underlying dementia may remain.

Patients with a dementia of depression tend to have a more rapid onset of memory impairment than patients with Alzheimer's disease; they often have a past or family history of depression; they fluctuate in functioning more during any day, week, or month; they give up more easily when challenged with a question; and they are more consistently depressed than are patients with Alzheimer's disease. (See also chapter 10.) These distinctions are subtle and often require extensive observation and evaluation; it is crucial that this be done to make the most accurate diagnosis.

Sometimes the distortions in thinking are rather dramatic. One older woman was "driving her husband crazy" with the conviction that "there was another couple living in the apartment with them." Her incessant monologues about the intruders and their habits exasperated her husband and puzzled family and friends who found her delusion inexplicable and bizarre. This was the most alarming of her many symptoms of depression. Disturbing thoughts such as this are often missed as symptoms of depression and are labeled as "crazy." When treated as part of the depression, they usually remit.

Delusions of illness, poverty, and jealousy are also encountered among the symptoms of depression. A 69-year-old woman, with no symptoms or risk factors, was certain that she was infected with the AIDS virus. One 79-year-old man was convinced that someone was rearranging or stealing some of his clothes and other belongings each night while he was asleep. An 81-year-old woman was convinced that her 86-year-old invalided husband was having a love affair with a widow in a nearby apartment. Both of these people were regarded by their family members and family physicians as "senile" and therefore hopeless. Both could be viewed psychodynamically as expressing or trying to cope with their generalized sense of loss in life, although in a disordered way. Not all delusions in older people are the result of depression, but that possibility should be considered since the available treatments for depression are so effective.

Hallucinations—hearing voices that give disturbing or private messages, seeing people or things that are not apparent to anyone else, smelling odors that are not verifiable by other observers—are unusual symptoms of depression and other psychiatric and neurologic disorders. They should not be passed off as just due to old age or to senility.

As at other ages, depressed older people tend to be self-blaming, pessimistic, and hopeless about the future and ever getting better. They may have forgotten when they last functioned well or see it as having been a long time ago. They may easily adopt the attitude that they are old anyway, "so what's the use of trying." They may lose sight of the people, relationships, and experiences that even relatively recently existed in their lives, and will again, if they can be successfully treated for their depressive symptoms. They may deny the positive personality attributes that they have had for all their adult years. They may actively seek a solution in suicide or may passively and unconsciously ignore health, nutrition, or safety so that an earlier death is made more likely.

Mrs. S. is an 80-year-old who was well and highly functional, involved in local politics, crafts, and a small business, until she sustained a heart attack, which resulted in some complications, a hospital stay of several weeks, and a recuperative period at home of several months. Shortly after the initial event she began to have extreme feelings of hopeless and worthlessness, dismissing any discussion of her lifelong work and her reputation as always being "the life of the party." She denied the value of her many relationships with friends, children, grandchildren, and others. The change in her outlook on life was dramatic and not at all consistent with the actual prognosis of her cardiac condition. She verbalized a wish to die. Her cardiologist became alarmed and referred her for treatment of depression.

Suicide

Suicide is more common in older people than in any other age group. The rate of suicide in white men increases with each decade until age 90. For women, the peak suicidal risk is in the immediate postmenopausal period. The population over 65 years (13 percent of the total U.S. population) accounts for more than 25 percent of the suicides committed. And when older adults attempt suicide, they are more likely to succeed than are younger people. Suicide attempts by older people should not be dismissed as gestures. They must be taken seriously; they always mean distress. Most suicides, at every age, are attempted by people who are depressed or are just mobilizing from a serious depression. In view of these data, family members should be alert to expressions of extreme hopelessness in their depressed relatives, and clinicians should seriously consider these in any evaluation of the depressed older adult.

Suicidal feelings occur at least occasionally and fleetingly in most depressed people (and maybe in most people), but the idea that suicide might be a relief from one's state of mind, a solution to great despair, is another matter. The actively suicidal state may be temporary or recurring and should be approached by the clinician as a serious symptom of a severe but potentially treatable depression.

Many of the vulnerabilities for suicide are the same as for depression, but there are also some special risk factors. Men are at greater risk than women; recent widowhood is a special risk factor, as are medical illness, living alone, alcohol and other substance abuse, and dementia. Most older people who commit suicide have visited a physician in the prior few weeks. Most have had an increase in physical complaints but do not necessarily mention depression or suicide. Most suicides seem impulsive, and there is often no warning of increased distress or desperation.

It is worth asking depressed older people if they feel as though life is not worth living. Have they thought about harming themselves, about suicide? How strong are the feelings or thoughts? Do they have plans to do it? Can they talk about the distress? The observer—family member, friend, or clinician—should be assessing whether the patient has the means to commit suicide. Is there a collection of pills or guns in the house? (Obviously these should be removed.) Is the person often alone?

Most people who are in great distress welcome the care, concern, and support of those around them; they are frightened by their feelings and thoughts and are usually willing to seek help. At times, however, the help of others must be enlisted to protect someone who is potentially dangerous to self but resistant to the idea of a psychiatric evaluation from an avoidable catastrophe. Family physicians, mental health professionals, or, as a last resort, the police should be called to assist in an emergency in which hospitalization is necessary to protect someone from suicide.

What about the terminally ill patient who expresses a wish to die? For many, with the ravages that come with advanced metastatic cancer, overwhelming pulmonary, cardiac, kidney, or other organ failure, incurable infections, totally disabling neurological conditions, and other end-stage diseases, it seems reasonable that they would want to stop treatment and die without further suffering. Many people are choosing to make provisions for such eventualities through advanced directives—living wills and durable powers of attorney for health care (see chapter 7). Those decisions are well considered at an earlier time of life and when there is no interference caused by depression or other mental status changes. That is different from suicide. Most older people with terminal illnesses who are cognitively intact and not depressed are not suicidal; they usually want the benefit of maximal treatment, until they die of the disease or its complications or until they are in a vegetative or comatose state.

The Process of Evaluation

It is easy to dismiss sad feelings as "just the blues." The people around a sad person tell him or her, "Just get busy with something," or "Pick yourself up, and everything will be fine." Everyone has blue days in response to a sad anniversary, an unhappy event or circumstance, or for no apparent reason, and the sad feelings subside in a few days. Depression means a persistent feeling of intense sadness for several weeks or more, accompanied by some of the signs and symptoms described. Depression in its milder forms may respond to support from family and friends, to ventilation from talk, exercise, good diet, socialization, and pursuit of activities of interest. The response depends on the causes of the depressive episode, the vulnerabilities of the individual, and the person's coping reserves. In any situation, these supportive measures should certainly be tried.

Most depressed older people go first to their family physician to whom they are drawn by familiarity, trust, and the frequent association of depression with physical complaints. No one should ever accept a physician's or anyone else's explanation that the depression is "just because of old age." Hopefully only few people hear that pronouncement. Depression is a medical-psychiatric disorder that should be evaluated and treated. Some older people have had prior contact with a psychiatrist or other mental health professional, and they may consult with this person directly. Others are referred by their primary care physicians to psychiatrists and other mental health professionals. Because of the complex interaction of medical and psychiatric issues, particularly in older adults, a careful assessment by an appropriate clinician is always required before any treatment is initiated.

The History

Since many people in the current generation of older adults think that "you have to be crazy" to see a psychiatrist or that such a professional cannot help anyway, there is often some reluctance to seek an evaluation, though the pain of depression is great. In addition, they may find it frightening to seek care for a "mental problem," particularly if it is affecting their ability to think, remember, or concentrate or if they feel hopeless and worthless. If the primary symptoms are physical, the patient can seek medical consultation and try to deny the psychiatric aspects. A supportive, caring friend, relative, or physician can be crucial to the success of the efforts to define and treat the problem at hand. The auxiliary person is not only an aid to the patient but serves as a source or corroborator of information to the clinician in situations where the patient, because of anxiety, memory difficulties, confusion, or denial, does not fully reveal the extent of the symptoms, family issues, or social environment.

The physician or mental health professional will ask many questions to get a complete history of the person and the difficulties, much as they would about any other presenting illness. They will systematically ask about:

- The chief complaint—a description, in the patient's words, of the major current problem or feelings with which the patient is dealing.
- The history of the present problem—a detailed account of everything related to the recent symptoms, dating back to when the person last felt reasonably well.
- The person's past medical and psychological history, including past significant symptoms, illnesses, surgery, hospitalizations, and medication use.
- The family history of medical and psychological problems; causes of death of close relatives.
- The person's social history—activities, interests, functional abilities, habits, and regular schedule.

The clinician will be particularly interested in the patient's activities of daily living—the extent to which the person performs the day-to-day tasks of maintaining himself or herself, his or her home, cooking, dressing, toileting, bathing, paying bills, using a telephone, driving a car, socializing, and to what extent these have changed in the recent months or years. This is a basic method of determining the extent and effects of the depressive symptoms. The clinician will wonder why this person is seeking help now. What has recently changed in this person's life? What has alarmed the patient or family?

The Physical Examination

Most mental health professionals who work with older people insist that a physical examination be performed before making a psychiatric or psychological diagnosis and treatment plan. This is usually done by the patient's family physician or internist in consultation with the psychiatrist, who may want to suggest a focus on certain aspects of the examination. Most psychiatrists do not do physical examinations on their patients but will suggest an appropriate physician to consult, if that is needed. Neurologists frequently are called upon to evaluate older patients who show signs and symptoms of dementia or depression. They are experts in the functioning and disorders of the brain and nervous system, and they often work collaboratively with mental health professionals.

The physical examination assesses the state of health of the person, with emphasis on possible physical disorders that may present with depression as a primary symptom. These include endocrine disorders, of which thyroid problems are the most common, and neurological problems, such as insufficient blood flow to the brain, small strokes, or brain tumors. Many of the last can be treated if diagnosed early in their course. The possibility of anemia, heart failure, chronic lung disorders, nutritional deficiencies, kidney failure, and various chronic infections is evaluated. In fact, almost any medical condition in older people may present with depression.

The physical examination focuses on the extent to which an ongoing depression may have weakened a person who has been suffering for weeks or months. The patient may have lost weight because of decreased appetite and may be malnourished. Depressed people may not drink enough fluids and can become dehydrated. The physical examination assists the psychiatrist in determining how many of the patient's physical complaints are based primarily on a physical disorder and how much they are exaggerated or caused by emotional reactions set off by the depression. Sometimes in older patients, increased physical symptoms mask the nature or extent of the depression. Finally, the physical examination can give the psychiatrist an estimate of the patient's ability to tolerate the effects of antidepressant medications that may be used in the treatment process and a baseline from which to judge the future effects of medications. For all these reasons, the physical examination is crucial to any workup for depression in the elderly, where the mix between mind and body functions seems so apparent.

The Mental Status Examination

The evaluation of mental status is best performed by a psychiatrist or other mental health professional. A geriatric medicine specialist, internist, or family physician will often make a good estimate of the extent of the depression; this clinician is usually the first step in the diagnostic process. The psychiatrist or other mental health professional—psychologist, clinical social worker, or psychiatric nurse—is a specialist in these disorders; he or she will usually do a more exhaustive assessment when consulted and will work collaboratively with the primary care physician. In keeping with a growing interest in the medical and psychiatric problems of older adults, there are now geriatric specialists in several of the mental health professions. In 1991, the American Board of Psychiatry and Neurology, the organization that certifies psychiatrists and neurologists, instituted an Added Qualification Certification in Geriatric Psychiatry. Approximately 1,000 psychiatrists in the United States and Canada are so certified. The psychiatrist or other mental health professional will not only assess the current state of the patient but will initiate treatment, follow the patient's progress over time, and monitor the beneficial and adverse effects of medications and/or other therapies.

The mental status examination is accomplished by observing and listening to the patient during discussions of the history and current status and by asking some specific questions. Several general areas are focused on during this evaluation.

The patient's *appearance* is observed from the initial contact and throughout the interview. Does he or she make eye contact? Is he or she anxious, agitated, unable to concentrate or focus on the questions or responses? Does the patient look sad? Is he or she pale? Is there apparent evidence of recent weight gain or loss? What does the patient's body language tell us?

The extent of the patient's depressed *mood* is assessed. Is it consistent during the interview or over several encounters? Is it appropriate to what the patient is discussing? Does the patient appear to be elated at times?

The patient's *thoughts* are evaluated in terms of the content and process of thinking. Are there particular concerns or preoccupations? Are the patient's thoughts dominated by recent or past failures, losses, guilt, sadness, or suicide? Does he or she make sense in describing those thoughts?

What are the patient's *strengths*—positive attributes and supports that might sustain him or her through a stressful period or provide a basis on which to draw in the treatment process? Does the patient have goals—something to look forward to? Can the patient appreciate past successes and better times? Many depressed patients forget that there were good times in the past and doubt they will occur again in the future. Does the patient have delusions, hallucinations, or obsessional ideas on which he or she is stuck or compulsions that he or she cannot stop performing?

Since many patients have or have had *suicidal ideas*, it is crucial that this area be probed. What are the ideas? Do they have suicidal plans? Have they attempted to act on those plans in the recent past? No patient first gets suicidal ideas because they are asked about, although some families are shocked that this subject is openly talked about, even by a psychiatrist. A psychiatrist concerned about the patient's suicidal risk may want to enlist the family's help in ridding the house of potentially lethal weapons and medications. He or she may ask the family to provide special monitoring or nursing while the patient is most acute or help to hospitalize a reluctant or frightened patient for whom hospitalization might offer protection and treatment.

The mental status examination next focuses on *cognitive or thinking functions*. This is particularly important in the older patient because the two major psychiatric problems of later life—depression and dementia—can affect the individual's ability to think, remember, concentrate, and use new information. By accurately evaluating these functions, the clinician can get valuable diagnostic clues as to the source of the problem. Some of the information will be obtained from the patient's responses during the history taking, and other material will be gained by a systematic review of specific mental functions. In some medical settings, it may be tempting to base a cognitive assessment of a patient on the conversational or casual parts of the interview. This is dangerous; people with well-honed and retained social skills may look and sound deceptively healthy until cognitive functions are more formally evaluated.

Clinicians note whether the patient is "alert"—that is, awake—or whether he or she is in a stupor or even semicomatose or comatose. If the patient is not alert, an immediate medical examination, usually in the hospital, is required to investigate the possible causes of this altered state of consciousness, called delirium. People who are primarily depressed or demented are nonetheless alert.

One of the basic areas of testing is orientation to person, place, and time. Does the patient know who the people are in his or her environment, where he or she is, and what the time (day, date, etc.) is? These functions may be somewhat impaired in relatively isolated people and also in people who are either depressed or demented. Too often this is where the nonpsychiatric clinician starts and stops the assessment of mental status. It must go further to evaluate cognitive status more completely.

Tests of memory include asking the patient to remember three words or names of objects, to repeat them immediately, and then to remember them three or five minutes later. The patient can be asked to recall recent stories in the news, current events, favorite television programs, or recent family occasions. Past memory is tested in the history-taking process and more formally by asking about schools attended, names of teachers and friends, dates of birth of children or siblings, and the names of recent presidents of the United States, starting with the present one. A patient may be asked to recite the months of the year backward.

All of these tests have limitations in that they have some cultural and socioeconomic biases. Experienced clinicians have a large repertoire of assessment tools and will vary the questions to use a relevant framework to evaluate a given patient. Some of the responses may have to be corroborated by a family member or close friend.

Concentration may be evaluated by asking the patient to count back by sevens from 100—giving the responses 100, 93, 86, 79, and so on. This also tests arithmetic ability. An easier task is subtracting threes from 20. Both memory and concentration are tested by having the patient repeat a series of digits forward and backward. The ability to think abstractly, a higher cognitive function, is tested by asking for the meaning of various proverbs, such as "No use crying over spilled milk" or "People in glass houses shouldn't throw stones." Another test of abstracting capacity is asking about ways in which certain items (say, a rose and a tulip) are similar or different from each other.

The mental status examination is an essential part of the evaluation. The information obtained must be integrated with other aspects of the assessment so that a more complete clinical picture can be obtained.

Laboratory, X Ray, and Other Special Tests

In view of the relationships between depression and other medical conditions, a complete evaluation of the depressed person includes a battery of laboratory tests to help rule out other medical conditions, to assess the extent to which an existing depression may have affected a person's physical functions, and to have a baseline in case treatment with medication is prescribed. If these tests have not been performed in the past six months, they must be repeated.

The laboratory workup usually includes a complete blood count (CBC), urinalysis, liver and kidney function tests, a thyroid profile, electrolyte levels (sodium, potassium, chlorides, calcium, and others in the blood), a check of vitamin B_{12} and folic acid, and a blood test for syphilis. In addition, it is useful to have a recent chest X ray and an electrocardiogram (EKG). The computerized tomogram (CT scan) and magnetic resonance imaging (MRI) of the brain are tests that help diagnose problems within the brain, such as tumors, strokes, blood vessel abnormalities, and other structural changes. At least in large urban settings in the United States, these tests are a part of the evaluation of neuropsychiatric conditions such as depression and dementia. They can reveal evidence of many brain problems but do not specifically indicate whether someone is depressed or whether Alzheimer's disease is present. There is no one test that is confirmatory of either of those diagnoses. More sophisticated imaging techniques, such as single photon emission tomography (SPECT) and positron emission tomography (PET scan), are research tools that may be able to be more specifically diagnostic at some time in the future.

Another part of the evaluation for depression may include some standardized questionnaire profiles. These screening tests are used to estimate the extent of depression or cognitive impairment and to obtain a numerical score that can be compared with later testing, to evaluate the effects of treatment. These include the Mini Mental State Examination,[*] the Geriatric Depression Scale,[†] the Brief Cognitive Rating Scale,[‡] and many

---

[*]M.F. Folstein, S.E. Folstein, and P.R. McHugh, "Mini-mental state: A practical method for grading the cognitive state of patients for the clinician," *Journal of Psychiatric Research* 12:189–198 (1975).

[†]T.L. Brink, J.A. Yesavage, O. Lum, *et. al.*, "Screening tests for geriatric depression," *Clinical Gerontologist* 1:37–43 (1982).

[‡]B. Reisberg, M.K. Schneck, S.H. Ferris, G.E. Schwartz, and M.J. deLeon, "The brief cognitive rating scale (BCRS): Findings in primary degenerative dementia (PDD)," *Psychopharmacology Bulletin*, 19:47–50 (1983).

others. More comprehensive neuropsychological testing is sometimes administered when there are specific diagnostic questions best addressed with such a battery.

All of these procedures may sound like an enormous amount of time, effort, and cost just to determine whether someone is depressed or to estimate a baseline of physical and psychological functioning. Because people are more diverse and complicated as they age, it is as important to do a thorough evaluation for depression as it is for diabetes or heart or kidney disease. Correct diagnosis and treatment is essential no matter which organ system is affected. Each part of the examination and each of the studies yields just one piece of information in a puzzle that the clinician attempts to assemble to reach a diagnosis and treatment plan.

The Diagnoses of Depression

Depression is a confusing and complex term, with different meanings for different people. It is used by some people to indicate they are having a bad day; it can mean "the blues," sadness over the death of a friend or neighbor, or the "down" feeling one has in recuperating from a medical illness. Some use *depression* to mean they "are not quite right" but not particularly disabled; they are able to function in their usual ways, and the sadness seems to abate after a few days or a week. This kind of depression, or dysphoria, happens at all ages and does not usually prompt a complaint to a professional unless it is repetitive. People who are transiently and mildly depressed may talk about their feelings to friends and family, work them out in various ways that have been useful in the past, or accept them as a part of life. Although everyone has brief ups and downs, we should be wary of dismissing persistent or pervasive sadness or depression as normal, particularly in the later years when it can have dire consequences. In this book, *depression* refers to a set of symptoms—a syndrome or disorder—that is disabling; it interferes with a usual state of well-being or with social or occupational functioning. *Well-being* and *adequate functioning* are subjective terms that refer back to a time when the person last felt well. A change in functioning or well-being over a period of weeks or months usually prompts people to seek help for themselves or their family members.

The estimated prevalence of depression and the diagnostic schema for older adults is somewhat in dispute. Several studies demonstrate that up to 15 percent of community-residing older adults have significant depressive symptoms; over 25 percent of patients hospitalized for medical problems are affected, and more than 40 percent of nursing home residents are depressed. The prevalence of the diagnosis of major depression is much smaller, in the range of 2 to 4 percent in the community and up to 20 percent in the nursing home setting. There have been problems associated with obtaining accurate epidemiologic data on depression in older people because of the quality of the test instruments, the study sampling techniques, and the subtleties of diagnosis.

Depression can be diagnosed categorically by using criteria that mental health professionals generally accept. That is, a given set of symptoms can be labeled with a recognized diagnosis. The diagnostic criteria are contained in the *Diagnostic and Statistical Manual of Mental Disorders*, often referred to as the DSM-IIIR. It gives psychiatrists and other health and mental health clinicians a common language for the many psychiatric conditions that affect patients. Having a diagnostic guide offers the opportunity for easy communication between professionals, allows for common schemes for developing and testing new treatments, and facilitates diagnostic and statistical research. A diagnosis assists the clinician in considering what might be the most helpful treatment plan for a particular person.*

Particularly in the elderly, an argument can be made for

---

*American Psychiatric Association, *Diagnostic and Statistical Manual of Mental Disorders*, 3d ed. rev. (Washington, D.C.: APA, 1987). The DSM-IIIR is the latest in a series of diagnostic manuals developed by the American Psychiatric Association over the past forty years. It will be superseded in 1993 by the DSM-IV, which will incorporate refinements in diagnostic categories, based on research and clinical use, since the last edition was published. The DSM-IV will be coordinated with the International Classification of Diseases (ICD 10), a compendium of medical diagnoses that is used worldwide.

adopting a spectrum approach to depression rather than a categorical one, as used in the classification manuals. This means that the clinician evaluates the depression on a scale from mild to severe and develops a treatment approach based on severity rather than on a specific diagnosis, such as major depressive episode or dysthymia. The ICD-10 and, perhaps, the DSM IV will incorporate a spectrum approach. Many older adults are quite functionally impaired because of depression, and they justify serious treatment, though they may not fulfill the criteria usually associated with major depression. The clinician should be aware of the specific DSM-IIIR diagnosis and also make an assessment based on a spectrum of mild to severe depression. The ultimate treatment decisions should be based on how impaired a patient's functioning has become because of depression, whether or not the person qualifies for a specific diagnosis.

Psychiatric diagnoses are commonly talked about by both professionals and the general public. They should not be regarded as accusations or labels but rather as general categories that have some usefulness in the clinical setting. Some of the categories most frequently used for depression in the DSM-IIIR follow. The depressive diagnoses are sometimes combined and referred to as either "affective" or "mood" disorders. They include: major depressive disorder, dysthymia, bipolar disorders, cyclothymia, adjustment disorder with depressed mood, and organic mood disorder. Within each diagnoses an estimate of severity can be made.

Major Depressive Episode

A diagnosis of major depressive episode is made when the patient exhibits five of the following nine symptoms or signs over a two-week period, nearly every day, and they represent a change from previous functioning; among the five, "depressed mood" or "loss of interest or pleasure" must be included:

1. Depressed mood, most of the day, nearly every day
2. Markedly diminished interest or pleasure in all or almost all activities

3. Significant weight loss or weight gain when not dieting or change in appetite
4. Insomnia or increased sleep nearly every day
5. Psychomotor agitation or slowing
6. Fatigue or loss of energy
7. Feelings of worthlessness or excessive inappropriate guilt
8. Diminished ability to think or concentrate or indecisiveness
9. Recurrent thoughts of death; suicidal thoughts, attempt, or plan

In the past, major depression has also been referred to as "psychotic depression" or "endogenous depression." Those terms imply a serious disorder with probably biological components. Although the depression may be triggered by real or imagined losses or upsets, the extent of the symptoms almost always seems out of proportion to the actual loss. It is as if some internal (endogenous) problem is magnifying the precipitating events, making them seem insurmountable. In spite of its seriousness, major depression can be treated, and the vast majority of patients improve or totally recover.

> Mrs. M. is a 79-year-old widowed woman who, until one year prior to consultation, was an independent and high-functioning person. She drove her car, played bridge weekly, attended church services, took care of her apartment, cooked, and was enrolled in a class at a local senior center. She had friends with whom she made social engagements, and she saw and enjoyed her children and grandchildren.
>
> Approximately eleven months prior to her visit to a geriatric psychiatrist, the carpeting in her apartment was damaged by a burst pipe in the apartment above hers. The immediate water problem was solved, but efforts to prevent staining of her carpet were unsuccessful. The carpeting was twenty years old, was well worn, and was due for replacement soon. Her family thought that she would be happy to know that an insurance company would largely pay to have her carpet replaced. They were wrong.
>
> Over the next three months, Mrs. M. became sad, teary,

and lethargic. She had difficulty sleeping at night, had decreased appetite, lost ten pounds, and seemed to lose interest in most activities she had previously enjoyed. She spent little time in her apartment, choosing to visit friends, sit alone in restaurants, or ask a friend to take her somewhere—anywhere. She stopped reading and complained that she could not concentrate on anything.

Mrs. M. became obsessed with the damage to her carpet and procrastinated when family members made efforts to help her pick out new carpeting. She said that her life was over anyway, so why should she get new carpeting, even though it was almost free.

After six months of symptoms, Mrs. M. agreed, at her daughter's urging, to see a psychiatrist for consultation, although she "didn't believe in psychiatry." Her symptoms of depression were extensive; the damaged carpet served as a focus for her feelings of loss and impending doom. She was treated with antidepressant medication and psychotherapy. She was able to reminisce about the good and bad times in her life and to cry about some things she said she had not talked about in twenty to twenty-five years. (Those "things" were as old as her carpet.) She responded dramatically to three weeks of combined treatment with psychotherapy and antidepressant medications. She resumed many of her activities and eventually picked out new carpeting just prior to the insurance company's deadline; she seemed increasingly content. In six months she was back to normal; she had difficulty remembering that she had been so upset, and she stopped seeing the psychiatrist.

Mrs. M. had the symptoms of a major depression six months prior to seeking help. Her sadness, loss of pleasure and interest in activities and people, fatigue, insomnia, loss of weight, feelings of worthlessness, and indecisiveness pointed to a major depression with potentially serious consequences. They represented a radical change from her prior level of functioning. Although she didn't "believe in psychiatry," she fully participated and responded successfully to the treatment.

Major depressions can be subtyped by severity (mild, moderate, severe, with and without psychotic features, such as hallucinations and delusions.) Depression can also be seasonal and melancholic, depending on the timing and nature of the symptoms.

Dysthymia

Dysthymia, formerly referred to as depressive neurosis and sometimes called "minor depression," is less severe than major depression. In dysthymia there is a chronic mood disturbance in which there is a generalized loss of pleasure and interest in all usual activities, but there are no psychotic features (hallucinations, delusions) that are sometimes a part of major depression. The specific DSM-IIIR criteria for dysthymia include the following:

1. Depressed mood for most of the day on most days for at least two years.
2. While depressed, at least two of the following symptoms are present: (a) poor appetite or overeating, (b) insomnia or oversleeping, (c) low energy or fatigue, (d) low self-esteem, (e) poor concentration or difficulty making decisions, and (f) feelings of hopelessness.
3. During the two years, no lapse of symptoms of two months or more.
4. No evidence of major depression during the two years.

The layperson and sometimes the nonpsychiatric clinician may have trouble distinguishing these diagnoses, and, in fact, there may be some blurring at the extremes of the syndromes. Dysthymia implies a chronic, less severe problem than major depression, but in the elderly, this disorder can be quite disabling. It is the most common form of depression at all ages. Dysthymia may be a lifelong problem and may be exaggerated by life events such as deaths, illnesses, and other losses. This diagnosis again raises the issue of depression as a spectrum disorder, extending from the mild dysthymia to the severe major depression. Vigorous treatment with psychotherapy and antidepressants may be necessary to deal with the loss of functional ability that can result from this problem, even though it is not designated as "major."

> Mrs. P. is a 72-year-old woman with long-standing feelings of inadequacy and low self-esteem and more acute feelings of depression and anxiety. While she recognized that some of these feelings were almost lifelong, life became more depressing to her following the recent deaths of two close friends on whom she had depended for over ten years. She felt sad, irritable, and teary-eyed and had more trouble sleeping than in the past. Although she generally felt "down," she occasionally enjoyed visits from her family and some old friends. She complained that people did not visit her enough. Although objectively fully competent, she worried about how long she would be able to take care of herself.
>
> Mrs. P. was physically healthy and took no medications except for an occasional tranquilizer. She walked almost every day in the neighborhood, although her distances had decreased. She said that she felt depressed and "revved up" at the same time. During the interview with a psychiatrist, she looked and sounded sad, and she primarily talked about her inadequacies and losses. There were no psychotic symptoms.
>
> Mrs. P. had been treated with a tranquilizer for what her physician thought was chronic anxiety. Although it made her feel less anxious, it also made her feel more depressed. After the diagnosis of dysthymia was made, Mrs. P. was successfully treated with an antidepressant medication and supportive psychotherapy. She began to focus more on her personal strengths, sociability, family ties, and her use of walking as an important outlet for negative feelings. After three months she described herself as "improved but not cured."

Bipolar Disorders

Bipolar disorders, previously known as manic-depressive illness, are less common than either major depression or dysthymia, but they must not be overlooked in the elderly. Bipolar disorders commonly arise in young and middle adulthood, but they may continue to recur into late life or even be diagnosed for the first time in the later years. "Bipolar" implies both manic and major depressive episodes, which occur periodically and last days, weeks, or months, with or without intervening level periods. Whether manic or depressive episodes predominate, there is usually a history of the other state somewhere in the patient's past.

Manic symptoms include elation or euphoria, hyperactivity, excessive spending of money, decreased need for sleep, agitation, irritability, grandiose or exaggerated ideas, and pressured speech. Many of these symptoms appear to be the opposite of depression, and, indeed, many of them are experienced as pleasurable by the affected patient. The disorder often results in poor judgment, impulsiveness, and erratic behavior and thinking. There appears to be some genetic predisposition to bipolar disorder, although life stresses can play a role in the onset of any particular episode. In the absence of other symptoms, older people with bipolar illness may be primarily agitated or irritable.

An 80-year-old retired lawyer was brought to a psychiatrist because of excessive spending and grandiose ideas that he was going to be appointed to the president's cabinet. He used the telephone at all hours of the day and night to call relatives to tell them that the announcement by the president would be occurring soon. After several weeks of his having little sleep, much activity and pacing, and writing checks for large amounts of money to various charities, his wife became alarmed. She had never seen him like this and thought that "something was wrong." The family physician did some tests to rule out medical conditions that could cause behavioral changes but found nothing.

When seen by the psychiatrist, the patient was flamboyantly dressed in stripes and plaids and looked younger than his 80 years. He talked loudly and rapidly and seemed almost unable to stop talking; his ideas were difficult to follow completely. He was irritable, could not concentrate on questions asked, and paced in the office. He felt that this consultation was a waste of time, and he needed to be near his telephone.

With some convincing from his family, he agreed to enter the hospital on the condition that a telephone would be available so he could "get the call."

People with bipolar disorder are more likely to have a family history of mood disorders, are more likely to have problems with alcohol abuse (sometimes in an effort to control the manic symptoms or to sleep), and are at greater risk of suicide than are people with depressive episodes alone. Bipolar illness is highly responsive to treatment with lithium, neuroleptics, and other medications. While treatment may be begun in the hospital, as soon as the patient is stabilized, outpatient treatment is desirable.

Other Diagnoses

Cyclothymia (bipolar II or hypomanic syndrome) is a mild form of bipolar disorder, with mood swings that do not usually significantly interfere with functioning. The patient may benefit from treatment, but usually this can be managed outside the hospital.

Adjustment disorder with depressed mood is a diagnosis made in generally well-adjusted people who have mild to moderate depression that is clearly related to a stressful event and that diminishes when the stress is eliminated.

Organic mood disorders are depressions or manic episodes that result from a temporary or permanent brain dysfunction or from a disorder elsewhere in the body that affects the brain. The symptoms resemble those detailed for manic and depressive episodes. Medications, strokes, endocrine abnormalities such as thyroid disturbances, infections, and other medical disorders may cause organic mood disorders.

The Treatment of Depression

Depression is one of the most disabling common medical problems to which people are vulnerable. It is also one of the most treatable. Ironically, it often goes untreated, either because it is misdiagnosed or not diagnosed or because it is accepted as part of the normal aging process. While we and our relatives seek consultations and second and third opinions for heart, lung, bowel, and kidney problems, we may not think of depression as a real medical problem that has real treatments. Untreated depression is one of the most painful illnesses at any age, with possibly dire consequences, including a life of gloom, feelings of impending doom, increased medical illness, and even death. Depression that is properly treated can add years of productivity and happiness to someone who had given up on those aspects of life.

The treatment of any medical disorder begins with the initial inquiry or contact. I have outlined the important aspects of an evaluation for a depressive disorder. The treatment usually follows that evaluation, often by the same clinician. Sometimes there are problems with older adults' complying with the idea and reality of treatment although they were willing to be assessed. The prospect of talking psychotherapy and/or medication often meets with significant resistance. The patient requires the support, sometimes the persuasion, and even the threats of family members and friends, as well as the conviction and encouragement of the clinicians who are consulted.

The Reluctant Patient

Today's older adults largely think of mental health professionals, particularly psychiatrists, as treating "crazy" people. "Surely I don't need someone like that. I'm not crazy. I'd be taking up their valuable time. They could be treating someone who really needs it." This is a common refrain from the resistant older patient. In all likelihood, future generations of elderly will more easily accept the significance of psychological issues in their lives, and treatment will be more acceptable for them to seek. Just in the last decade, increasing numbers of older people have seen the possibility that psychiatric treatment may be helpful to them, and they more readily accept that prospect, either because they are in great pain and are desperate or because they have a more enlightened view of psychological aspects and difficulties of life. There have been increasingly successful efforts by various professional organizations to destigmatize psychiatric disorders among older adults so that evaluation and treatment will be considered acceptable. In spite of these efforts, less than 20 percent of older adults who could benefit from the treatment of depression avail themselves of it. Older people may fear that they will be labeled "crazy" and possibly be institutionalized against their will. Others fear the effects of treatments such as medications, electroconvulsive therapy, or even talking about their problems. These fears can be anticipated and addressed by family members and professionals.

A spouse, adult children, or friends feel caught in a bind when they recognize that a loved one shows signs of a psychological problem, possibly depression, and that person will not cooperate, or actively resists, in efforts to get help.

> Mr. T. is a 74-year-old businessman who retired from full-time work at the age of 70 and had worked part-time until one year ago. In the last year, since his complete retirement, he did not want to get out of bed on most mornings, was lethargic during the day, and occasionally said that life was not worth living. He would easily start crying, for no apparent reason or with seemingly minor provocation, and generally appeared to be sad. He was less careful in his grooming and dress, occasionally forgetting to wash his hair, brush his teeth, or change his shirt for several days. Mr. T. complained that his memory "was gone," and in fact he forgot the names of close business associates he had known for many years. His wife noted that his appetite was markedly decreased, and he appeared gaunt, as if he had some chronic disease. He was irritable, barking at her when she asked him a question or made a suggestion.
>
> Mr. T. rejected his wife's suggestion that he go for a medical checkup to evaluate his condition. He angrily said that his condition was "old, and that's all there was to it." His children sought a psychiatric consultation to help them figure

out what to do about their father. The psychiatrist pointed out that their father's presentation could be caused by a variety of medical disorders, including possible neurological and psychiatric problems. A complete medical evaluation was necessary to unravel the mystery.

Because of the family dynamics, it was decided that one of Mr. T.'s daughters and one son would confront him with their concerns and help him get to a physician to determine the reason for his personality and other changes. They were prepared to be greeted with hostility, but surprisingly Mr. T. responded to their firm appeal, and he made an appointment to see his internist.

The key factors in helping someone like Mr. T., who is highly resistant to seeking an evaluation and possible treatment, are firm confrontation, expression of genuine concern, and respect for the autonomy of the potential patient. Confrontation is best done by close relatives or friends who have the most clout with the prospective patient. It should be done by a small group of two to four confronters. Mrs. T. had already been labeled by him as a "nag," and he "was tired of hearing her complain" about his change of personality. Besides, he knew how to manipulate and scare her with his anger. She had lost her credibility with him. Mr. T.'s children had seen the changes in their father over the past year but did not live nearby and were not involved with him on a daily basis. He had always respected his son and daughter for the "sensible ways they conducted their lives." They were the obvious confronters, and it required both of them.

The prospective confronters may find it useful to meet with a mental health professional, in advance, to organize their ideas, and to plan a general approach. Mr. T.'s son and daughter were encouraged to express their concern to their father supportively but to persuade him to seek help for what they regarded as a potentially serious problem, which had changed him drastically. They gave Mr. T. graphic examples of the ways in which he had changed and declined. They mentioned his lack of desire to see his grandchildren in the last six months and cited his recent disregard of his appearance, when he had previously been a fastidious and rather sharp dresser.

Respecting his autonomy as a mature person with a significant problem, they expected him to follow through with a plan to get some answers to this problem. He could choose the route. They offered to assist if he wanted help. They were unyielding against his protests that "everything is under control." Mr. T. saw his two children as partners in this effort with him; they had conveyed their caring and determination in a firm, supportive manner, which left no doubt in Mr. T.'s mind that they respected him, were concerned about him, and were not going to be manipulated. In the end, he appeared relieved.

Most resistant older adults finally welcome this approach, which is based on the intervention technique that Alcoholics Anonymous has used successfully. But it is not always as easy as it was with Mr. T. A small number of people will not be persuaded, even by the best-prepared, most firm, concerned family members. Sometimes a family physician can directly intervene, and sometimes the family may have to await further deterioration, when involuntary hospitalization may be the last resort.

Once Mr. T. was able to accept the idea of getting some help, it became apparent that he had been very frightened to find out what was wrong with him. He seemed to mellow and accepted his wife as a helping person. With the involvement of her children, Mrs. T. felt more actively supported, became less anxious, and was consequently less threatening to her husband. She accompanied him to his appointments with several physicians. Mr. T. was diagnosed as having a major depression and was treated with medication and psychotherapy. Within two weeks, his mood began to improve gradually; after three weeks, he made plans to see some of his former business associates and to enjoy his leisure time with his wife.

Treatment Options

- What is treatment or therapy for depression? Is it a lifelong commitment?

- Are the medications addicting or dangerous?
- Does "talk therapy" work?
- Isn't electroshock therapy dangerous and barbaric?
- Can I be treated in a doctor's office, or must I go into a hospital?

These are among the commonly asked questions about treatment for depression. This section gives an overview of the treatment options and answers these questions. Patients and families are urged to discuss treatment plans with the psychiatrist working with them and to get reasonable answers to questions of concern. Psychiatry is not mystical or mysterious; it is increasingly scientific. Clinicians draw on a significant and growing body of research concerning the treatment of mood disorders. Depression is disabling and life threatening; sensible and vigorous treatment is called for.

There are dozens of possible treatments for depression. The major categories are psychotherapy ("talk therapy") of various kinds, medications, and electroconvulsive ("shock") therapy. All of these are effective in certain situations. Some are used alone and others in combinations.

PSYCHOTHERAPY. *Psychotherapy* is a general term for "talk therapy" and includes several techniques with different theoretical bases. Some people wonder why they "can't just talk to a good friend about their problems; friends understand each other and have similar problems." For some problems, talking with friends can be very helpful. Many difficulties have been solved and much "psychotherapy" has been done over a cup of coffee or tea with a friend. But a trained psychotherapist is more objective, has dealt with many people with difficult problems, and is not as personally involved in the situation at hand. The therapist may help the patient recall things he might not be able to with a friend and to identify themes and patterns in behavior, thoughts, and feelings that people closer to the scene may not see.

Classical psychotherapy is described as dynamic or psychoanalytic and has its roots in the work of Sigmund Freud in the early

1900s. Although Freud was pessimistic about the capacity of older people to change through psychotherapy, several of his disciples recommended intensive psychotherapy as a treatment for older patients and found it successful. In the last twenty years, psychoanalysts and other psychotherapists have increasingly and successfully used psychoanalytically oriented techniques for the elderly, even the oldest old. Dynamic or psychoanalytically oriented psychotherapy involves the patient's talking about "what's on his mind" and, to the extent possible, expressing thoughts and feelings in as uncensored a manner as possible. The therapist or analyst remains as neutral and objective as possible and helps the patient understand the anxieties, conflicts, and pain inherent in the psychiatric disorder. Implicit in the psychoanalytic theory is the notion that early childhood experiences and traumas play a large role in later dysfunction. The therapist uses the patient's memories, dreams, free associations, and feelings that develop between patient and therapist (the transference) to understand the patient's problems. By clarifying and interpreting those understandings to the patient, the therapist promotes insights and eventually changes in thinking, feeling, and behaviors. To many, the technique sounds mysterious, unscientific, formal, and inefficient, but it often produces changes that are therapeutic to many people. Most dynamically oriented psychotherapy practiced today, while having its origins in Freudian theory, is not as rigidly practiced so that recent events and current real-life problems are dealt with extensively, at the same time that older themes are considered.

The psychoanalytic technique is often not selected by older people because it requires a commitment of years rather than months of therapy, it is expensive, and usually it is applicable, by itself, only for people with mild to moderate depression. In the treatment for older adults with major depressive episodes where there are expressions of hopelessness, worthlessness, sleep changes, weight loss, and suicidal thoughts, psychotherapy should be combined with medication. Many older adults feel the press of time and want to get on with their lives without delay. They see extensive therapy as stalling. Others want to keep down what has been covered up for years and do not want to engage in a therapy in which old feelings and thoughts will be explored. Some elderly view psychotherapy as an opportunity to look at the past in order to understand the present better.

For the older person with moderate to severe depression diagnosed with a major depressive episode or bipolar disorder, I recommend and use a combination of psychotherapy and medication. The psychotherapy uses some of the principles of the dynamic approach, especially in the therapist's attempt to understand what the patient had endured, as well as principles of supportive psychotherapy. *Dynamic* implies the understanding of why and how people feel and think about themselves and their relationships, in both the past and present. *Supportive* means the acknowledgment and fostering of the patient's strengths and useful defenses that have served the patient well in the past and can be mobilized to master difficult situations in the present. It is neither necessary nor desirable for everyone to delve into all aspects of the past to attempt to understand all the psychological details of one's life. This issue should be weighed by the therapist and considered with the patient during the evaluation and as treatment continues.

Talking is an important aspect of any treatment for psychological pain. Although it may not be curative, it is almost always relieving. One's lifelines of relationships, experiences, and inherent capabilities provide a backdrop for the talk of a supportive therapeutic experience. These assist the patient and therapist to think about the individual's strengths and weaknesses, recurrent themes and new concerns. The therapy can utilize reminiscence techniques in which patients are encouraged to review their life experiences to draw on assets that may have been overlooked and to come to terms that may not have been worked through in the past. Depressed older adults can well use the support offered by an empathic therapist who is "on the patient's side" and helps him or her build on the strengths that have worked well for the patient in the recent and more distant past. The therapist conveys an optimism that the psychological problem is treatable. The approach to the older patient requires a flexible clinician who understands the dynamics of normal aging and the complications that depression may bring to that time of life.

Psychotherapy that includes a comprehensive approach, integrating the positive factors in normal aging, the benefit of one's lifelines, combined with medication, produces considerable relief for most people in weeks to months. Most patients stop psychotherapy when they are symptomatically improved, but some find it a continuing learning and sustaining experience. Others return at crisis points in late life, when support, new exploration, or medication is needed. Patients who primarily benefit from medication will need infrequent visits to a psychiatrist or other physician who monitors them for treatment and adverse effects and has the opportunity to make dosage adjustments and deal with occasional crises.

Other popular and effective individual treatments include cognitive and behavioral therapies. While I have focused on individual psychotherapy, group and family techniques are also used with older adults.

Cognitive therapy helps people look directly at the negative thoughts they have about themselves and the world around them in order to correct the self-defeating behaviors that are the result of those ingrained thoughts. It attempts to correct long-held thinking habits that perpetuate negative views and promote depression. The therapist uses logic and persuasion to correct the patient's negative view of reality. Patients may have thoughts such as, "I'm no good" or "I'm stupid," that color their views of themselves, particularly in stressful situations. Through cognitive therapy, the patient attempts to recognize the occurrence of these negative thoughts and to correct them, so that they are no longer automatic. Cognitive therapy has been effective in treating people with mild to moderate depression but should not be used without adjunctive medications in cases of severe major depression and bipolar illness.

Behavioral therapy attempts to change dysfunctional behaviors in depressed patients and focuses little on thoughts and feelings. Patients and family members are encouraged to list behaviors that are symptomatic or associated with the depressive problems, and a regimen is devised to gain mastery over those behaviors. Techniques such as desensitization, positive reinforcement, assertiveness, and relaxation training are used. The therapist functions as a trainer or coach to help the patient effect a change. This approach is widely used in hospital and outpatient settings and appeals to many patients who can follow the prescribed structured guidelines it offers.

Many skillful therapists use a technique that includes aspects of dynamic, supportive, cognitive, and behavioral approaches, depending on the needs of the patient. It is crucial for the therapist to review the course of therapy as it proceeds, to modify treatment strategies, and to seek consultation from another professional where appropriate.

Group psychotherapy can use any of the techniques mentioned and also includes elements of socialization and activity-oriented and educative approaches. Group therapists frequently use a combination of these techniques. A group may contain five to ten patients and one or two therapists. Although many patients fear sharing their feelings, thoughts, and behaviors with strangers, that obstacle is usually easily overcome, and most people find that the group experience is supportive and conducive for expression and change. It offers ventilation, positive reinforcement, and the opportunity for correction of cognitive and other distortion by other patients, who soon get to know each other well. Group therapy has the practical advantage of usually being less expensive than individual therapy, another inducement for older adults with limited financial resources.

Family therapy involves the identified patient and one or more family members' meeting with the therapist at the same time. There are many theories, techniques, and schools of family therapy, but generally all explore problems within the family system. By better understanding communication patterns and existing problematic ways of relating, the therapist and family members attempt to find more successful ways of relating within the family. With an older patient, family therapy may involve primarily the spouse and the identified patient, but it often includes adult children, grandchildren, and other significant people in the patient's life. Family sessions may be particularly useful when the patient is not entirely forthcoming, when the nature of family interactions and communications is not otherwise revealed, when the depression is related to family interactions or specific events, or when family dynamics function to maintain the depression in one or more of its members. Some older people, feeling uncomfortable because of cognitive changes or personality characteristics in the psychotherapy sessions, may want a spouse or family present to help them discuss issues, remember details, or provide support in an unfamiliar endeavor.

There is an array of adjunctive treatments that can be helpful in the therapy of mood disorders in the elderly. With milder depressions, they may, with or without some form of psychotherapy, be the only treatments required. In more severe depressions, adjunctive treatments may facilitate psychotherapy and pharmacotherapy. Some of these are regular exercise, as prescribed by family physician; increased socialization and pursuit of activities of particular interest; and art, music, dance, writing, and other forms of expression. Work, paid or volunteer, can sometimes serve as an adjunctive treatment, particularly when the loss of work is a significant precipitating factor for the depression. The therapist must attend to some of the practical issues that are a part of the older patient's life, including recreation, interests, activities, living arrangements, finances, work, family relationships, medical problems, and others. These are powerful factors, for better and for worse, in the treatment process.

With all types of psychotherapy with the older adult, it is crucial that the therapist be someone who understands the issues involved in normal aging and has experience working with the specific problems of later life. The belief that older people, drawing on the resources of their lifelines, can make changes no matter how old they are, is vital to a successful treatment.

MEDICATIONS. The development and use of specific medications over the past thirty-five years has revolutionized the treatment of depression at all ages, including people in the later years. Serendipitous discoveries and the results of basic and applied research in the neurosciences have brought new understandings of the biological bases of depression that have yielded effective treatments. University medical centers, federal and private research institutions, and the pharmaceutical industry are all involved in ongoing research and clinical trials to understand and treat mood disorders better. While medications are not panaceas, when judiciously prescribed, they can make the difference between someone being able to function well and not being able to function at all. Sometimes medications are life-saving, and at other times they relieve the more disturbing symptoms of depression enough so that people can use psychotherapy and other psychosocial treatments more effectively. People who have moderate to severe major depressive or bipolar illnesses will usually require medication at some time in a successful treatment program.

Older patients who are depressed may have considerable resistance to taking medications. They may feel they can get better without drugs or they may fear dependency on them. Because of the probability of significant relief of symptoms, antidepressant medications are vital to the care of moderately and severely depressed people, and resistances to them should be supportively confronted by family members and professionals involved in their care.

The following medications are most frequently used for the treatment of affective disorders:

Cyclic and other newer antidepressants
Monoamine oxidase inhibitors
Lithium
Stimulants
Benzodiazepines (and other "minor" tranquilizers)
Neuroleptics ("major" tranquilizers)
Sedative-hypnotics (sleep-inducing drugs)

All of these medications are effective in their various roles in the treatment process, and all also have adverse side effects. In choosing a particular drug, the prescribing physician weighs the effectiveness of a medication against its risks and side effects. He or she will use past experience in treating patients with medications and what is known from clinical and research studies. The presence of adverse effects may determine whether a patient will agree to begin and then stay with a treatment. The physician should warn the patient and family about possible side effects and suggest ways of dealing with them. Before prescribing any medication for depression, the physician will have performed or will have access to a report of the medical history, physical examination, and any laboratory data and other tests that have been accumulated in the evaluation process. These are crucial in making decisions about the choice of specific medications and in monitoring side effects. In addition, no physician would want to be treating a depressive disorder alone when an equally or more severe additional medical problem also existed.

Cyclic and Other Newer Antidepressants. The tricyclic antidepressants have been the bulwark of pharmacotherapy for depression from the 1960s. The group is so named because the chemical structures of the compounds include three rings. There are more than a dozen different tricyclic antidepressants; all are effective, but they vary in the extent and nature of their side effects. There is an increasingly large group of newer, nontricyclic antidepressants. Individual patients find one medication more effective or more laden with side effects than another, and while some general patterns exist, the diversity of biological characteristics in the older population makes it difficult to predict which medication is right for which patient. Sometimes there is a need to try a second or third drug to achieve the most effectiveness with the least side effects. In general, the beneficial effects of medications far outweigh the difficulties, and it is worth tolerating the short-term discomfort that may result from side effects for the longer-term relief.

As with pharmaceuticals for other medical illnesses, most medications used for psychiatric disorders are available in both brand names and generic names. The generic name is the chemical name of the drug itself, while the brand name is given by a particular pharmaceutical company that manufactures and sells it. Generic medications are usually less expensive and can often be substituted for a brand name. Sometimes a brand name is preferred by a prescribing physician because the generic drug may have been found to not be as effective. This issue should be discussed with the physician and pharmacist.

The tricyclic antidepressants used most commonly with the elderly are nortriptyline (Aventyl, Pamelor), desipramine (Norpramin, Pertofrane), imipramine (Tofranil), amitryptyline (Elavil, Endep), and doxepin (Sinequan, Adapin). These drugs generally increase the amount of brain chemicals (neurotransmitters) that regulate the transmission of nerve impulses at the junctions (synapses) of neurons in the brain. The two neurotransmitters most involved are norepinephrine (noradrenalin) and serotonin, although others may be affected. Each antidepressant alters one or more of the neurotransmitters to a varying extent. While there may be some beneficial effects (usually improved sleep) in less than a week, maximal treatment effects do not occur for several weeks. The most common side effects of this class of medications are drowsiness, dryness of the mouth, constipation, increased heart rate, difficulty urinating (more common in men), and lightheadedness when standing up quickly from a sitting or lying position. Some of these side effects abate within several days to a week, but it is not uncommon for the physician to suggest alternative medications if the first seems to have too many side effects or the patient cannot accommodate to them. Nortriptyline and desipramine tend to have fewer side effects than the other tricyclics.

In the past decade, several newer nontricyclic antidepressants have been developed. Trazodone (Desyrel) was one of the first in this group. It is highly sedative, as well as having antidepressant properties, and is useful in a nighttime dose for people with significant sleep problems. Bupropion (Wellbutrin) is a nontricyclic antidepressant that has been used successfully in the elderly. It can cause restlessness, anxiety, and agitation early in the treatment. It should not be used in patients with seizure disorders.

Fluoxetine (Prozac), paroxetine (Paxil, Seroxat), and sertraline (Zoloft) are members of a group of drugs that specifically increase the amount of serotonin available at the synapses of neurons in the brain by selectively inhibiting the usual reuptake of the neurotransmitter in the synapses between brain cells (neurons). The resultant increase in serotonin at the brain cell (neuron) junctions facilitates an antidepressant effect. They have not been studied extensively in the elderly but offer promising prospects for the treatment of depression in older people. This class of drugs is highly effective and generally has fewer of the side effects common to the tricyclics. Possible adverse effects reported for this group include agitation, insomnia, and gastrointestinal disturbances. Because these medications are highly effective with fewer side effects, they are relatively easy for nonpsychiatric physicians to prescribe. This is usually beneficial, since more people will receive early treatment for depression. In many situations, however, a consultation and an assessment by a psychiatrist may be advisable, particularly if the patient is severely depressed, significant adverse effects develop, or if a patient does not improve within several weeks.

Patients should not be discouraged if the first medication is not effective or the side effects are greater than expected. Each person has individual biological and psychological characteristics, and care always needs to be individualized. There are a large number of effective antidepressants from which to choose, and each of them has different characteristics; patience is necessary for the patient, family members, and physician as attempts are made to find the right medication regimen for a specific person. The selection of an antidepressant for any one patient is a question of finding the most effective medication with the fewest adverse effects. Patients with certain underlying medical problems, such as heart, liver, or kidney disorders, may need special monitoring when taking antidepressants. Because antidepressant medications are so highly effective, it is worth making great efforts to be treated properly with one of them.

Older adults generally need smaller doses of medications than do younger people because the aging process changes the rates of absorption, metabolism, and excretion of most drugs, although some people, even some older adults, may require rather larger dosages for a therapeutic response. Patients and physicians should be prepared to increase the dosages slowly as appropriate for the individual. Most of the antidepressant medications can be taken in a single dose, either in the evening, for most of the tricyclics, and in the morning for some of those that are more activating, such as fluoxetine. The once-daily dose is a distinct advantage to elderly patients, who are often taking several or even many medications on complicated schedules.

After a patient begins taking an antidepressant, maximal therapeutic effect is not achieved for two to six weeks. After several days, sleep often improves, and the patient may feel calmer. Gradually the patient will experience more interest in activities and will have an improved appetite and a generally improved mood. Physicians usually monitor the effects of the medications by the clinical response of the patient. At times, they may check the amount of drug in the patient's system by doing a blood test. They may want to perform other tests of kidney, thyroid, or liver functions as treatment proceeds. A patient who responds well to treatment feels "like a new person," "like I've been brought back to life." With optimal treatment, the patient will feel back to normal. Antidepressants are not "uppers" and should not result in symptoms of elation or euphoria, which are not desirable and should be reported to the prescribing physician.

Antidepressant medications must be taken daily, over a period of at least months, so that a high enough and consistent level of medication is achieved in the blood. They are not effective on an occasional dosage schedule or on an as-needed basis, as can aspirin for pain or some tranquilizers for anxiety symptoms. The decision to stop antidepressants after a good result is sometimes difficult. Once a patient starts taking these medications, it is desirable to continue for at least six months to a year before the dose is tapered at the recommendation of a physician. They are not addictive. Few people like taking medications, and a difficult problem for the physician is the patient's desire to stop the drug after a brief period of improvement. The patient may say, "After all, I feel so good now, why should I continue taking a drug?" Just as patients with hypertension need lengthy, sometimes indefinite, periods of treatment, so do patients with depression. The decision to stop a medication should be made with the physician, and the dosage must be carefully tapered over several weeks, under his or her supervision. Neither the patient nor family member should change dosage or type of medication without the advice of the prescribing physician. Similarly, the use of alcohol or medications for other medical illnesses should be checked with the physician. Antidepressants are highly effective and generally safe medications, but they can be potentially dangerous when used carelessly.

Monoamine-Oxidase (MAO) Inhibitors. The MAO inhibitors are a separate class of antidepressant medications that increase the availability of neurotransmitters in the brain. They inhibit an enzyme that metabolizes those brain chemicals. The MAO inhibitors are effective medications for the treatment of depression. Especially in the elderly, they are generally regarded as secondary choices, after the tricyclics and other newer serotonin-enhancing drugs have been tried. Some people have remarkable responses to these medications after being unsuccessfully treated with the tricyclics and other drugs. The MAO inhibitors require that the patient observe certain dietary and medication restrictions to prevent serious side effects. The commonly prescribed MAO inhibitors are phenelzine (Nardil), tranylcypromine (Marplan), and isocarboxazid (Parnate).

Lithium. Lithium is one of the miracle drugs of the twentieth century. Introduced in the 1960s and popularized since the early 1970s, lithium is a chemical element similar to sodium and potassium. It is vital to the treatment of bipolar disorders and recurrent depression. Lithium is highly effective in treating people in the manic phase of bipolar disorder, as well as in preventing the ups and down of people with a history of the disorder. It functions to stabilize their moods. It is prescribed as lithium carbonate (Eskalith, Lithane, Lithobid, Lithonate) or lithium citrate

(Cibalith). In 70 to 80 percent of people suffering with manic-depressive symptoms, lithium provides a permanent remission as long as the medication is continued. It is highly effective in leveling the unstable moods of people referred to as cyclothymic—having cyclical mood swings that are not as extreme or intense as those with bipolar illness. Lithium is also useful to treat patients who have chronic or recurrent depressive episodes (without manic phases). Any person with significant mood swings that interfere with optimal functioning should be tried on a course of lithium unless there are medical reasons that contraindicate its use or unless the patient or a family member cannot be trusted to administer the medicine as prescribed. Lithium can be combined with neuroleptics and benzodiazepines (tranquilizers) in patients with a manic disorder and with other antidepressants when depression is prevalent. Psychotherapy is often combined with medication treatment in bipolar patients because of the interpersonal, family, and occupational havoc this disorder can bring. In fact, treatment with lithium often allows the patient to be more receptive to a talking therapy approach.

Because it must be carefully monitored and because it is associated primarily with bipolar disorders, many people, including some in the medical profession, think of treatment with lithium as an extreme measure. It is not. After some preliminary laboratory blood tests and an electrocardiogram (EKG), the patient is started on a small dose, given orally, two or three times per day. As with other medications, dosages for the elderly are usually smaller, and the physician should be aware of other drugs or medical illnesses that might be factors in the treatment. Lithium treatment necessitates periodic blood tests to monitor the level of lithium in the bloodstream. The first checks need to be done after a few days and then weekly for several weeks. After the dose is stabilized, blood tests should be done monthly, and after several months, even less frequently. The blood tests can be done at any doctor's office, laboratory, or hospital and are not major impositions compared to the enormous benefit derived from this excellent treatment. Therapeutic blood levels generally range from 0.5 to 1.5 nanograms per milliliter of blood. In the elderly, in order to minimize side effects, we aim for levels close to the lower end of the spectrum. Recent research and clinical experience point to the possibility of using even lower blood levels for maintenance treatment. The administration and monitoring of lithium should be done by a psychiatrist or other physician who is experienced in using the drug, particularly with the elderly. Patients for whom lithium is effective will probably have to take it for the rest of their lives to prevent the recurrence of symptoms.

Side effects of lithium are minimal, and if monitored properly there are almost no complications. Lithium is actually a safer drug, particularly for the medically ill, than the commonly prescribed tricyclics. Some patients complain of weight gain, muscle spasms, and mild tremors. Maintaining the lowest possible effective dose helps to minimize or eliminate these adverse effects. Lithium can induce a decrease in thyroid functioning, and this must be routinely monitored; these changes are reversible with thyroid medication or upon discontinuation of the lithium. When levels of lithium in the blood are too high, confusion, slurred speech, loss of coordination, and drowsiness may occur. Patients who take diuretics for hypertension or heart disease need special attention when taking lithium, and the prescribing physician will monitor these people more closely. Patients who take lithium should maintain a normal diet, with adequate fluid intake.

People who have been successfully treated with lithium point out that while they were manic, they may have felt euphoric and powerful, but they were also impulsive, out of control, and potentially dangerous to themselves. It is a challenge for psychiatrists and other mental health professionals to demonstrate that negative effects of the disorder require treatment in the face of the patient's feeling "so good." Lithium is not prescribed often enough in the older adult population. When used appropriately, most patients are exceedingly grateful for the symptom-free years that lithium treatment allows. When lithium is not well tolerated by a patient, there are other mood-stabilizing medications that have been found to be effective in some bipolar patients, including clonazepam (Klonopin), carbamazepine (Tegretol), valproic acid (Depakene), and valproate (Depakote, Epival).

Stimulants. Although not true antidepressants, the stimulant drugs, of which methylphenidate (Ritalin) and dextroamphetamine (Dexedrine) are the most popular, have a role in activating lethargic, apathetic patients who are just beginning tricyclic therapy or who cannot tolerate or are unresponsive to other medication treatments. Stimulants have been used for decades to treat children with attention-deficit hyperactivity disorder. In those situations, they work, paradoxically, to calm the children and help them better concentrate. While there are few clinical research studies that show their efficacy as antidepressants over time, clinicians have found them to be helpful in the treatment of some medically ill older patients with significant depressive symptoms. They are given in small doses early in the day so as not to interfere with nighttime sleep. They have few side effects and are effective within days. Stimulants are generally prescribed for short-term use. Potential but rare side effects include insomnia, decreased appetite, agitation, and rebound depression when discontinued. Stimulants also have a role as enhancers of tricyclic antidepressant therapy.

Benzodiazepines and Other Minor Tranquilizers. The benzodiazepines and other minor tranquilizers are antianxiety medications, primarily prescribed for symptoms of subjective nervousness, tension, and agitation. The benzodiazepines are the most popular subgroup of antianxiety drugs and are represented by diazepam (Valium), which has one of the longest periods of activity, clonazepam (Klonopin), an intermediate-acting drug, lorazepam (Ativan), alprazolam (Xanax), and oxazepam (Serax), which are shorter acting, and many others with varying periods of activity. They have been used to treat generalized anxiety disorders, as well as specific syndromes of panic disorder, posttraumatic stress disorder, and phobic disorder.

While many of the benzodiazepines can cause depression as a side effect, alprazolam (Xanax) has been prescribed as an antidepressant in people who cannot tolerate the tricyclics. With the advent of the newer serotonin-enhancing antidepressant agents, alprazolam is prescribed less frequently for depression. Buspirone (Buspar) is a nonbenzodiazepine, which is used for generalized anxiety and is thought, by some physicians, to have some antidepressant effects, particularly in higher doses. It is not used extensively as a treatment for depression, although may prove to be effective for people with a mixed anxiety and depression syndrome. Lorazepam (Ativan) is extremely effective as an antimanic treatment, and is often used with lithium in bipolar patients.

There is a significant overlap between anxiety and depression; approximately one-third to one-half of depressed patients have a coincident anxiety disorder, and future diagnostic schemes will likely have a category for a mixed anxiety-depression diagnosis. Some physicians prescribe antianxiety medications with antidepressants for patients with "anxious depressions." It is interesting to note in this regard that several antidepressants have been found to be useful in the treatment of specific anxiety disorders. Clomipramine (Anafranil), a tricyclic, is a major pharmacological treatment for obsessive-compulsive disorder (OCD); fluoxetine (Prozac) and sertraline (Zoloft), two of the serotonin-enhancing antidepressants, are also effective for OCD. Imipramine and other antidepressants are used successfully for panic disorder. Various MAO inhibitors that are now available are used for anxiety disorders, and others, specifically for the treatment of anxiety disorders, are being developed.

The benzodiazepines are most useful for the treatment of anxiety states. They have been widely prescribed, and many have become household names. Unfortunately, sometimes people with depression with or without a component of anxiety have mistakenly been given benzodiazepines as a primary treatment by physicians who have not made an accurate diagnosis. These drugs can often make the depression worse, and if taken for a long period of time, they may be difficult to discontinue. The longer-acting benzodiazepines, such as diazepam, tend to accumulate in the bloodstream of older people and are sometimes responsible for confusional states in patients who are already somewhat cognitively impaired or are recovering from medical or surgical illnesses. When judiciously used and monitored, the benzodiazepines and other antianxiety drugs have a role in the treatment of depression in the elderly when significant acute anxiety or agitation that does not respond to an antidepressant alone is present or as an adjunct for patients with alcohol or other substance abuse disorders.

Neuroleptics ("Major" Tranquilizers). This group of medications is highly effective in treating the severe agitation and psychotic symptoms—hallucinations and delusions—that may accompany a major depression or bipolar disorder in the elderly. An antidepressant and a neuroleptic are frequently combined for the treatment of a major depression with psychotic features, a delusional depression. Although the risk of adverse effects, such as dryness of the mouth, constipation, blurred vision, urinary retention, and movement disorders, is increased with these combinations, the therapeutic benefits are significant. The two types of drugs result in remissions that would not be possible with either one alone. Because of the risk of involuntary movement disorders, such as tardive dyskinesia, neuroleptics are prescribed for older depressed patients only when they have a severe delusional depression or when accompanying agitation is not controlled by other means. The neuroleptics, given once or twice per day, often result in sedation; thus, they can be used to treat the sleeplessness that often accompanies a severe depression. The neuroleptics most commonly used in older adults are haloperidol (Haldol), thioridazine (Mellaril), fluphenazine (Prolixin), thiothixene (Navane) and molindone (Moban).

Sedative-Hypnotics (Sleep-Inducing Drugs). Except for short-term use of several days to two weeks, I do not generally recommend the use of sedative-hypnotic medications (sleeping pills). (See also chapter 4.) Insomnia is distressing, but its treatment does not lie solely in the taking of potentially dangerous and addicting drugs. Insomnia is a complex problem; it is an aspect of normal aging for some people and a symptom of several disorders. Older people spend more time in bed and sleep less soundly, with an increased number of awakenings during the night. While there is probably no decrease in total sleep time, older people tend to have decreased nighttime sleep plus some napping.

In the last two decades, we have learned a great deal about the physiology of sleep and now have the knowledge and skills to make more rigorous diagnoses of sleep disorders. It is crucial to assess a sleep problem fully in order to have a better chance of treating it successfully. Certain sleep disorders, such as sleep apnea (disrupted breathing during sleep that produces multiple awakenings and consequent daytime sleepiness), are more common with increasing age. Anxiety and depression are two common psychiatric causes of insomnia. Various medications, alcohol, caffeine, pain, and medical conditions such as urinary problems, and cardiac, pulmonary, and other disorders also may cause sleep disturbances. Before prescribing a medication for sleep, the physician should counsel the patient about good sleep hygiene, including regular bedtimes and wakeup times; daily exercise; avoidance of stimulant drugs, caffeine, and alcohol; avoidance of excessive evening fluid intake; comfortable bed and pleasant surroundings, free of noise or odors; and use of bed for sleep and sex only. Those who cannot sleep should use the time awake for another activity—reading, listening to radio, watching television, writing letters, paying bills—out of bed, if possible.

Sleeping pills are dangerous drugs. They are habit forming, lethal in overdose, particularly when mixed with alcohol or other medications, and they are depressants. Barbiturates, the favorite sedative-hypnotic of some physicians who were trained in an era when they were more popular, and their patients, are specifically contraindicated for all of these reasons. If short-term sleep-inducing medication is necessary, there are several relatively safe drugs that can be used for days to a few weeks. These include chloral hydrate, antihistamines, and some short-acting benzodiazepines. These should be administered under the care of a physician, not borrowed from friends or relatives, and used primarily for acute medical or psychological stresses that may cause insomnia. Virtually all sedative-hypnotics produce some degree of tolerance, with higher doses required with longer-term usage.

For chronic insomnia that continues in spite of attempts to observe good sleep hygiene and a careful assessment of the specific sleep problem, home remedies such as drinking warm milk and others that individuals have found to be effective can be tried. When anxiety or depression is a factor in causing insomnia, a relatively sedating antidepressant such as trazodone or amitriptyline may be prescribed for nighttime use. Patients do not develop tolerance to these antidepressant medications.

Combinations of Medications. As psychiatrists have relied more on medications for the treatment of depression and with greater sophistication in the neurosciences, innovative treatment techniques have developed, which include the use of combinations of medications after one or more drugs have been used alone. Many of the medications described have been used in a variety of combinations. In addition, thyroid hormone, some anticonvulsants, propranolol, stimulants, and others have been used to augment or enhance the effects of the antidepressants.

ELECTROCONVULSIVE THERAPY (ECT). The idea of ECT ("shock therapy") is frightening to most laypeople, evoking fears of primitive torture or at least the horrors of *One Flew over the Cuckoo's Nest*. In fact, ECT is one of the most effective treatments for severe depression and may be life saving in certain situations. It is almost always administered in a hospital setting, particularly with the elderly, and the modern techniques used make it safe, humane, and effective, with minimal side effects.

Although in most situations, treatment is first attempted with antidepressant medications and psychotherapy, ECT is often more effective in the severely depressed older adult. ECT works quickly—usually within a week or two—while medications may require several weeks to be effective. ECT is particularly useful when the patient is extremely regressed and withdrawn, is not eating, is dangerously suicidal, or is tortured by the psychotic symptoms of delusions or hallucinations. When a patient is medically ill and antidepressants are contraindicated, ECT may be a safer treatment to use.

ECT is usually indicated for an acute depressive episode. Unlike antidepressant medications, it has little utility in the prevention of future episodes. Thus, patients who are treated with ECT are often maintained on antidepressant medications after an acute episode. ECT can be used effectively for repeated depressions, and many patients come to prefer it to other treatment options.

ECT is administered in an operating, recovery, or other emergency-equipped treatment room after the patient receives a short-acting anesthetic and a muscle relaxant drug. An electrode or small metal disc is applied to one or both temples, and an electrical current is briefly given from a special machine. Because the patient is under the influence of a muscle relaxant, there is little discernible convulsion, except for muscle contractions in the hands and feet, which last less than a minute. The patient is allowed to wake up and usually experiences some confusion and/or memory loss for a few hours. Treatments are repeated two to four times per week for a total of five to twelve treatments.

Some patients suffer impaired memory for some weeks or even months, but this is usually significant and long-lasting only in people who are previously cognitively impaired. There is a small incidence of heart rhythm disturbances, headaches, and rare fractures when there is preexisting osteoporosis. These risks have to be weighed against the sometimes life-saving benefits that can result from ECT when it is prescribed for patients with severely disabling depression.

An 82-year-old man had been treated for a fever and urinary tract infection on the medical ward of a university hospital. From the time of admission, he refused to eat and stopped speaking; he was maintained on intravenous fluids during the ten days of evaluation and treatment. The nurses taking care of him thought he was depressed and said he behaved as if he was going to die. He had a history of previous depressions and severe heart disease, which precluded the use of antidepressant medications. Stimulant drugs in small amounts produced no effect, and he was resistant to psychotherapy.

After his cardiac problems were stabilized he refused further treatment. He revealed to a nurse that he thought he would die during that hospitalization and hoped that would happen. He had visions that "the Lord is coming to take me." Efforts to convince him to try electroconvulsive therapy were in vain until he developed an attachment to an older woman who cleaned the medical unit and who reminded him of his deceased wife. He seemed to have a new reason to live, and with the nurses' encouragement he agreed to have ECT. After three treatments, his mood lifted considerably, his vigor slowly increased, and he became more verbal and coherent. He suffered minimal memory loss but was able, after three additional treatments, to return to his apartment in a retirement center and to function more independently than he had in a year.

Hospitalization

Most people with depression can be treated as outpatients; they do not require hospitalization. There are, however, several major reasons to seek hospitalization for inpatient treatment: the need to perform extended diagnostic evaluations, particularly in the elderly, when medical issues may complicate the diagnosis and treatment of depression; to use new or intensified treatments in a highly supervised and controlled setting; to protect a person from suicide, homicide, severe agitation, or potentially dangerous behaviors that result from psychotic thinking; or to respond to family exhaustion or concern about the patient; or to provide medical or nursing care that the outpatient clinician and caregiver at home can no longer provide because of the increasing severity or chronicity of symptoms.

The hospital provides physicians with a valuable option in the diagnosis and treatment of depression in the elderly. The consideration of hospitalization is carefully made, because of the emotional and financial consequences. Although often frightened by the prospect, the patient and family are usually relieved that they are receiving more intensive care than can be provided in an outpatient setting. Sometimes partial hospitalization or day treatment is available and suitable for many patients. In these settings, the patient spends most of each day in an extended outpatient facility and goes home to a family member, friend, or other caregiver in the evening. The cooperation of family may be necessary in assisting the patient to get to and effectively use partial hospitalization successfully, and the patient cannot be at risk for doing harm to self or others.

Family Issues

Beyond dealing with the reluctant patient, a family member or close friend can be vital to the successful treatment of depression, or any other major medical disorder in the older person.

> Mr. F. had been an active, healthy person until his wife died three years ago. Now, at the age of 75, he still went to his business daily, but "had no zest" for business. "What's the use, she's gone; I have no one and nothing to work for," he would say. He was unable to prepare meals, and he did not clean his apartment or have it cleaned by anyone else. He had not bought new clothes in years and stopped driving his car for no particular reason. He lost ten pounds, slept poorly, and worried about dying, sometimes wishing he could. He was irritable, complaining about physical symptoms that his physician could not diagnose, and about his children and grandchildren who did not visit enough. He felt hopeless about the future and enjoyed little in his life.
>
> His children and grandchildren did not think he was much fun to be with. As a matter of fact, they tried to avoid him. He was interested only in himself, and he had been such good company before his wife's death. His depression affected his

children and grandchildren who struggled with their love for him, their anger and disappointment with him, and their worry about what would ultimately happen to him. They cared for him and wanted to help, but they did not want to be consumed by his neediness. They felt guilty that they could not do better for him, and they yearned for the person he had been to them. Would he ever get better? What were the effects of treatment? Would their lives be determined by his depression?

These issues are typical of what a psychiatrist hears from family members about their relatives with depression and, to some extent, about other disorders as well. All families are stressed when a member becomes disabled. It is more complicated when that person is a key member of the family, the leader, the dominant force. The depressed older person can become regressed and childlike, dependent, irritable, and demanding, and the family experiences sadness, anger, guilt, and fears that are common when attempting to cope with a close relative who has a chronic debilitating illness. A vicious cycle can be set up in which the patient alienates the people who can be of the most help to him. He wants the benefit of his family's support, but they run from his dependency, sadness, complaining, irritability, and criticism. He has not taken on a new personality; he is a victim of an illness—depression—which in addition to its symptoms, exaggerates his worst personality characteristics. If one or more family members can step back a bit and see this person as a medically or psychologically ill individual, requiring treatment, the family may be able to mobilize its strength cooperatively to assist in the therapeutic process. It is essential for the family to see depression as a disorder that is treatable, much as are other medical problems.

The family has potentially vital roles in the treatment process. One or more family members are usually the first ones to *observe* the patient as depressed. While the patient may be able to cover up at work or in some social situations, it is a family member or close friend who knows that there has been a gradual or dramatic change in functioning, mood, behavior, and relationships. It is the family that usually *initiates* or assists in initiating treatment. Most older adults are pushed to get treatment by a concerned spouse, child, grandchild, or close friend. Sometimes this requires rather forceful confrontation. Once started, the patient needs *support* to stay in treatment, to come to appointments, to take medications, and to follow instructions about diet, exercise, socializing, and other activities. Usually the family serves a crucial role in supporting the treatment process over the hurdles of "I feel better so why should I go to see a doctor, and why take medicine?" or "Why tolerate the side effects" of one or more medications that are tried.

An episode of severe depression may alarm the patient and family to think about the advisability of a change in living arrangement. Maybe the patient needs more support. Should he or she move in with a child or into an assisted-living residence or other adult accommodations? An episode of depression, even a severe one, can be treated successfully and need not signal the beginning of the end, nor does it mean that major changes are automatically necessary. The patient may well return to his last best level of functioning. On the other hand, a depression may alert the patient and family to a need for some changes, immediately or in the near future, that might make the life of the older person more comfortable and more functional. The family can assist in such transitions.

The patient and family members almost always feel better once someone else, particularly a clinician, is involved in the situation and, better yet, once the patient begins to feel and act more as he did before he was depressed. The family and friends play an essential role in their support, but they must also be wary of being overwhelmed by the needs of a depressed person. Everyone has a tolerance for such things, but it is important to be aware of when that point of feeling abused is reached. It is important for family to set limits so they can continue to be available.

The patient may be seen by a mental health professional with a family member, particularly a spouse, to get a full picture of the patient's functioning. The therapist can also use the family member as an auxiliary in the treatment process. Sometimes family therapy is recommended so that all or part of the family can be seen together to work out stresses, support family strengths, better understand the ways in which the family functions, and appreciate the place of the patient in the family system. The therapist may focus on communication patterns within the family, on family history and dynamics, strengths and weaknesses, and on grossly dysfunctional elements. The therapist alleviates the stress somewhat by entering the family system, observing, clarifying, and supporting elements of healthy family functioning. He or she also educates and, in the case of depression, may explain the biopsychosocial aspects of the disorder, the genetic information that is known, the treatment options, and the prognosis. The therapist gives the family permission and opportunity to discuss difficult feelings and thoughts with each other. Every family has its rituals, values, and, perhaps, some sense of spirituality, which serve to keep it functioning. The therapist looks to use and reinforce all the positive elements within the family to treat the identified patient maximally and gain from the family strengths.

The person without a family or close friends usually has considerably more difficulty when physical or emotional problems occur in later life. After an illness necessitating hospitalization or while undergoing extensive outpatient treatment, special arrangements must be made thoughtfully by the medical staff to ensure adequate care, at home or in a rehabilitation care center. Visiting nurse services and social service agencies can fill certain needs for care. More isolated people, who have lived their later lives alone and have no family, have often worked out an emergency support system with friends, neighbors, a local merchant, clergy, congregants at a church or synagogue, an attorney, an assisted-living residence, or a nursing service. Some discover the value of retrieving old friendships and renewing family relationships as they realize what they may face if disabled, without someone to assist them. Others who are totally alone have great difficulty getting help other than on an emergency basis and offer the biggest challenge for preventive medicine of various kinds and early treatment of disabling illnesses, such as depression. Even at a later age, those people might consider, when they are healthy, the potential crisis created by an illness and find community or institutional supports that are viable supportive options for them. One robust and healthy 82-year-old widowed woman feared that at some point she might need more care than she now did. She had no immediate family and did not want to rely on distant relatives. She researched and then selected a continuing-care community in the city where she lived. She rented an apartment and knew that if she required greater nursing or medical care, it was available on the premises. This was an enormous relief to this proud and independent person.

The treatment of depression is complex in the older adult, involving a range of possible therapies that can be use alone or in combination. The clinician must be versatile, flexible, knowledgeable, and skillful in working with an aging population. Because of the often complex physical and psychological issues in older people, the physician should make use of other medical consultants, when necessary, to give the patient optimum care.

Depression is not a part of normal aging. It is a serious, potentially fatal, clinical disorder that can be successfully treated in the vast majority of affected people. Proper treatment must be sought, attempted, and vigorously pursued without the prejudice that an older person is "entitled" to be depressed, merely because of age. Depression is often a chronic disorder; treatment may have to be continued to maintain maximal functioning well after the patient is substantially improved, in order to attempt to prevent relapses and recurrences.

10

Coping with Alzheimer's Disease and Other Dementias

Mr. M. is a 70-year-old man who was brought to the geriatric psychiatry clinic by his wife because he had increasing inability to remember the names of people and of common household items over the past year. He was confused about who had telephoned or visited the house, was not sure of the day of the week or month, and had stopped reading the newspaper. Initially, the changes in Mr. M. were denied by family members. Then they thought he was just forgetting more, like some older people do, with little consequence. Maybe they were part of his difficulty adjusting to retirement. Mr. M. had retired from a successful business three years earlier and was an avid sports fan, rarely missing a local sporting event and reading the stories each morning in the newspaper. Recently he announced that he "wasn't that interested" in sports and the news in general, and so he did not want to see the newspaper. Over the most recent six months, the changes in his memory could no longer be adequately explained as due to normal aging. On the day prior to the clinic visit, he lost his way on a walk in the neighborhood. He was evaluated for the possible diagnosis of dementia.

The term *dementia* means an impairment or loss of mental function. To psychiatrists, neurologists, other physicians, and mental health professionals, it means a category of disorders of the brain in which there is a progressive loss of intellectual function as brain cells die at a faster rate than they normally do in the course of aging. Dementias are organic brain disorders; there is structural or chemical damage to the brain that causes gross cognitive impairment. People with dementia typically and progressively lose the ability to remember both new and old information; eventually all recall is affected. They become disoriented and confused and lose the ability to perform daily tasks of living. As the disorders progress, there is a gradual loss of neurological and psychological functioning, which eventually encompasses all facets of physical and mental life. The term *senility* has also been used to describe this deterioration, particularly in older people. In the light of the increasing amount of scientific information that has been accumulated about dementia over the past two decades, more specific diagnoses have been introduced to try to dispel the notion of senility as a ubiquitous event of late life and to differentiate among the many possible diagnoses of dementia.

Senility has been used in the past to mean an expectable, inevitable mental failure that occurs to almost everyone as they age. This is incorrect; severe memory failure is *never* a part of normal aging and should not be accepted as just a part of growing older; dementia is a disorder of catastrophic proportions. Although the causes of most forms of dementia have not been determined, it is known that there are various pathological changes in the brains of people with these disorders; although these changes are not obvious until postmortem autopsy, they are clearly different from normal aging. The term *senile* is to be avoided because it is too generic and conveys an erroneous view that most people eventually lose the ability to think clearly. *Senility* falls into the same wastebasket as *nervous breakdown,* another term used by some people but that has little meaning or specificity in a diagnostic sense.

Dementia is one of the organic mental disorders described in the *Diagnostic and Statistical Manual* (DSM-IIIR) of the American Psychiatric Association. It is characterized by a memory impairment, often beginning with deficits in short-term memory but soon including longer-term memory as well. In addition to the memory impairment, there may be one or more of the following problems in cognitive functioning: (1) impaired abstract thinking; (2) impaired judgment; (3) language disturbances (aphasia), difficulty in performing tasks or using familiar objects (apraxia), and a lack of ability to recognize objects (agnosia); and (4) personality changes. There is a disturbance in work and/ or social activities and relationships, which may be barely perceptible early in the disorder, particularly in people who are bright and socially adept prior to the onset of symptoms. As the disorder progresses, the patient with dementia is increasingly unable to perform complex (financial matters, shopping, cooking, driving, use of telephone) and then even basic (dressing, grooming, eating, toileting) activities of daily living. An accurate history from family members, and by direct observation, of changes in a patient's activities of daily living are among the best indications of functional ability and the extent to which there is deterioration in patients with dementia. The deterioration in pertinent functions is also relevant to the extent to which, and under what circumstances, a patient can be managed at home by family caregivers. When they carefully think about cognitive changes in loved ones, family members are often able to give a history of the evolution of dementia in a given patient, over a significant period of time.

Mr. M.'s wife and son, on further questioning, remembered that he seemed confused and had difficulty setting up the Christmas tree almost two years ago; that was something he had done in the same way for over forty years. They also recalled that there were a few instances, about two years ago, when he had trouble following a conversation in which he would have normally been an active participant. There was one other episode around that time when he wanted to cook his favorite recipe for potatoes but appeared not to know what to do with the potato peeler. These several incidents had been passed off at the time, but now it was obvious that there was indeed a progression in his initially subtle symptoms.

Delirium, like dementia, is an organic mental disorder that causes confusion, disorientation, and memory loss. It is different from dementia in that most patients with delirium have some change in their level of consciousness; they are drowsy, stuporous, semicomatose, or comatose. They are not alert and fully awake as are patients with dementia. The delirious patient, in addition, has difficulty with attention, has disorganized thinking, often speaks incoherently, may be agitated, has visual hallucinations (such as crawling insects that are not there), sleep-wake cycle disturbances, and increased or decreased psychomotor activity.* Delirium is usually caused by a medical problem, such as congestive heart failure, kidney or liver failure, substance abuse and withdrawal syndromes, overdoses or reactions to certain medications, and other disorders that produce a systemic effect. Symptoms develop over a short period of time—hours to days—and may fluctuate during the length of a day. A form of delirium is called *sundowning,* a syndrome in which patients, often hospitalized or in other institutional settings, become agitated, disoriented, and confused in the late afternoon and evening. This is thought to be due to environmental and diurnal physiological stimuli that affect particularly vulnerable patients and produce a relatively time-specific form of delirium. Patients with delirium require immediate medical attention to ascertain the cause and to attempt to institute treatment.

Age-Associated Memory Impairment

As people age, starting even in the late 20s or early 30s, there is a noticeable decrease in their ability to remember some things. The loss is usually for recent memory and includes an inability to recall a particular word or the name of someone that had been previously known. There may be forgetfulness for information, such as where one parked the car or placed an item in the house. There is slowed retrieval of other kinds of memories, such as the name of that person you know so well who is approaching you at a party. Most people in most situations can recall the needed name or word spontaneously in one or several minutes, some-

*American Psychiatric Association, *Diagnostic and Statistical Manual*, 3d ed. rev. (Washington, D.C.: American Psychiatric Association, 1987).

times with the help of techniques such as reviewing the alphabet, various mnemonics, associations in one's mind to related situations or people, or reviewing one's schedule and path since an item was misplaced. It almost seems as if the needed name or situation is "on the tip of your tongue" and jumps back into your mind. While forgetfulness of this kind, referred to as age-associated memory impairment (AAMI), usually gets somewhat worse with age and is quite frustrating, even bothersome, particulary for people who were always proud of their excellent memories, it does not usually progress to dementia and does not significantly affect social or occupational functioning.* It can produce considerable anxiety in social or work situations, however, as words cannot be quickly retrieved. Most people acknowledge and understand this kind of memory problem because it is so common in the general population. Many are successful in trying to practice techniques to make retrieval easier. Some studies show that 5 to 15 percent of people with AAMI may develop significant memory failure later in life. Some people see this as an independent syndrome, others as the beginning of the continuum of memory dysfunction. There is considerable debate in the scientific community as to whether this condition is part of normal aging, a prelude to more severe memory impairment, and/or a treatable condition in its own right for which causes will be found and behavioral and medication regimens developed. As part of large-scale research efforts to study aspects of dementia, several research institutions and pharmaceutical companies are investigating potential treatments for AAMI. To date, none has been impressive in preliminary testing.

Diagnoses of Dementia

Although Alzheimer's disease is the most common, most studied, and most well-known form of dementia, there are several dozen related disorders that must be considered in the evaluation pro-

---

*T. Crook, R.T. Bartus, S.H. Ferris, *et.al.*, "Age-associated memory impairment: Proposed criteria and measures of clinical change—Report of the NIMH Work Group," *Developmental Neuropsychology*, 2:261–276 (1986).

cess when a patient has severe memory impairment, disorientation, and confusion. Mr. M.'s history and presentation, in the case example, is typical of someone with Alzheimer's disease, but the diagnosis cannot be made without ruling out other causes of dementia and disorders that cause changes in mental status. For example, many of Mr. M.'s symptoms could have been caused by a severe depression, an eminently treatable disorder.

One way to categorize the dementias is by the system or organ of origin. One group consists of *primary* dementias; the origin of the disorder is in the brain itself (such as Alzheimer's disease). The other dementias can be described as *secondary,* originating in other organs of the body (such as thyroid disease) or as the result of systemic or bodily disease (such as AIDS) (see table 10–1). To date, the cognitive impairment that results from primary brain diseases is not definitively treatable. In those situations, the goal is to treat the symptoms that accompany dementia and to help the patient and family maximize existing functional ability and cope with the catastrophe of brain failure. Since the secondary dementias are largely the result of disease elsewhere in the body and many of those disorders are treatable, to a great extent those dementias are potentially treatable and reversible; their correct diagnosis, when possible, is crucial to reversing the cognitive disturbance.

TABLE 10–1

The Diagnoses of Dementia

Primary Dementias	Secondary Dementias[a]	
Alzheimer's disease	D	Drugs (medications)
Parkinson's disease	E	Emotional (depression)
Pick's disease	M	Metabolic (sodium, potassium, body
Multi-infarct dementia		fluid abnormalities)
Huntington's disease	E	Endocrine (thyroid, pituitary, adrenal)
Jakob-Creutzfeldt	N	Nutritional (vitamin B_{12}, folate);
disease		normal pressure hydrocephalus
	T	Tumor; trauma; toxins
	I	Infections (AIDS)
	A	Arterial (vascular)

[a]Mnemonic courtesy of J. Yesavage, M.D.

Alzheimer's disease accounts for approximately 50 to 60 percent of the cases of dementia. The next most common form of dementia is *multi-infarct dementia* (MID), which causes 20 to 25 percent of the cases of dementia, with some patients demonstrating pathological evidence of both Alzheimer's and MID. Previously this disorder was lumped with other forms of senility and sometimes referred to as hardening of the arteries. It now appears that the hardening of the arteries, presumably because of arteriosclerosis, does not in itself produce dementia. Rather, MID is usually the result of multiple small strokes in the brain in sufficient numbers and in critical areas, causing the death of multiple small areas of brain cells, so that dementia ensues. Hypertension and cardiac rhythm disturbances play roles in causing this disorder. The clinical course is variable, depending on the timing, number, and place of the strokes. A stepwise pattern, with plateaus and exacerbations, has been described in which there may be long periods of stability punctuated by periods of dramatically increased disability. There may be some discrete neurological signs and symptoms and more psychiatric instability with depression, anxiety, and paranoid delusions than in some other forms of dementia. Control of hypertension, diet, and exercise may be helpful in preventing further strokes. Research is being conducted to examine the possible role of a number of medications already used in various cardiovascular disease (calcium channel blockers, angiotensin converting enzyme (ACE) inhibitors, and others) to see if any have a role in preventing or treating MID. Psychotropic medications, including antidepressants, benzodiazepines, and neuroleptics, can be used to treat psychiatric symptoms of agitation and depression that may occur in the course of the dementia. Many of the issues relating to the care of patients with Alzheimer's disease are also relevant to those with multi-infarct dementia.

Parkinson's disease is a neurological disorder resulting from damage to an area of the brain known as the substantia nigra. The cause of the damage is unknown, but it results in a decrease in the production of dopamine, a neurotransmitter vital to normal brain functioning. The most prominent symptoms include those of a movement disorder characterized by a resting and pill-rolling tremor, shuffling gait, rigidity of the extremities, and a masklike appearance of the face. Patients with Parkinson's disease are treated with l-dopa (levodopa), a precursor of the neurotransmitter dopamine, and other drugs in combination, to increase dopamine levels in the brain. Depression, probably related to effects of the brain disorder, is a common complication of Parkinson's disease, and between one-third and one-half of patients become demented during the course of the illness. The treatments for the movement disorders of Parkinson's disease do not improve the dementia that is often a complication. The relationship between the dementia of Parkinson's disease and Alzheimer's disease remains unclear. Whether the dementias are variants of the same disorder or two distinct diseases, with similar courses, is still in question.

Other secondary, potentially treatable or reversible forms of dementia are important to assess. Although they may account for only 10 to 15 percent of the cases of dementia, making an accurate diagnosis and instituting proper treatment in these cases can be the difference between a potentially normal life-style and one spent in nursing or custodial care. Physicians, mental health professionals, and the general public must guard against quickly diagnosing every case of memory impairment as an incurable form of dementia when other possibilities exist.

Medications for psychiatric and other medical illnesses may cause cognitive impairment that is symptomatically indistinguishable from Alzheimer's disease. While antihypertensives, cardiac anti-arrhythmics, H_2 antagonists for peptic ulcer disease, beta-adrenergic blockers such as propranolol, anti-inflammatory drugs, tranquilizers, and others are among the most common offenders, all medications taken by an older person with dementing signs and symptoms should be suspect as a cause of the mental status changes. Because most older people are taking several medications, the interactions of them may be the causative factor of a secondary dementia.

Mr. P., a 69-year-old man, was taken to a hospital emergency room after he was found wandering around on a snowy night, clad only in his underwear and muttering something about his dog. He was alert but confused, disoriented to time, place, and person, and unable to give his address, but he did declare that he was an attorney. He gave an incomplete medical and social history but alluded to taking several medications for various disorders. He was evaluated with medical, neurological, and psychiatric examinations, and except for hypertension, there were no apparent acute medical problems. His local physician was contacted and a better history was obtained. In fact, the patient had taken four medications for several years for a cardiac arrhythmia, gout, and hypertension. Approximately two months prior to this episode, a new medication had been added to the regimen to treat his cardiac problems better. He was admitted to the hospital with the presumptive diagnosis of Alzheimer's disease.

Mr. P. became agitated when told that he would not be able to manage at his home anymore and needed nursing home care. He was then given a neuroleptic medication (major tranquilizer) to deal better with the agitation. None of his original medications was changed during the hospitalization; rather, the neuroleptic was increased in dosage as he became more verbally upset at his invalid status.

Mr. P. had no immediate family, but a niece, visiting him from another city, was shocked to see him in his present state, just three months after he had argued a case in the Supreme Court. She questioned the diagnosis. A consultant was called in to review the case and pointed to the fact that he had not been tried off his medications or even at reduced levels. Although he needed to be medicated for several medical problems, a short trial off the medications while he was being monitored in the hospital would be safe. When the medication that had recently been added was removed, Mr. P.'s confusion gradually remitted, and within a month, he was back to his prior condition. The diagnosis of Alzheimer's disease was incorrect. Mr. P. had suffered the effects of a toxic reaction that mimicked the symptoms of Alzheimer's disease.

This case, although unusual, is not rare. Medications, either newly started or taken for many years, may precipitate a dementia syndrome. It may be due to changes in the metabolism of certain drugs at some point in aging and/or due to the mix of several drugs. It is easier to track down and cure this kind of dementia than it is some of the others.

Psychiatric disturbances, especially depression, can produce a syndrome reminiscent of a dementing illness. Previously referred to as pseudodementia, this is now called the *dementia of depression*. Although it may indicate that the patient in fact has some early signs of a primary dementia, the most severe symptoms of dementia in these cases respond dramatically to antidepressant therapies. Patients with metabolic disturbances, including abnormal levels of sodium, potassium, or calcium and other mineral elements, may have a reversible dementia, which responds to correcting the salt/fluid balance. Thyroid and other endocrine abnormalities, especially hypothyroidism, a decrease in thyroid function, may produce signs and symptoms of dementia that are indistinguishable from primary brain failure. Patients with mental status changes secondary to metabolic or endocrine abnormalities respond quickly to treatment for the underlying problem. Normal pressure hydrocephalus is an uncommon but important neurological disorder that causes dementia, usually accompanied by urinary incontinence and gait or balance problems. This unusual triad of symptoms alerts the clinician to a form of dementia caused by an impairment in the absorption of cerebrospinal fluid in the brain and resulting increased collection of fluid around the brain. When diagnosed early, the resulting dementia may be reversed by a surgical procedure that shunts the excess fluid from the brain into the person's circulatory system, thereby relieving the excess pressure on the brain.

Evaluating Patients with Dementia

Every patient with memory failure and other symptoms of confusion, disorientation, and personality change should be fully medically evaluated as outlined for the assessment of depression. (See chapter 9.) Medical, personal, social, and family histories, from the patient and from a close relative or knowledgeable friend, are obtained to track the changes in functioning from the time the patient was last perceived to be entirely well and to become familiar with all possible factors involved in the patient's forgetfulness, including whether other family members have had the disorder.

A careful medication history must be taken of medications prescribed, bought over the counter, borrowed from, and shared with spouse and other family members. Certain classes of medications are most likely to cause cognitive changes that can mimic Alzheimer's disease and other forms of dementia, but every medication, alone and in combination with others, should be suspected of causing mental status changes in an older person. No patient should change the dose or discontinue a medication that may be causing cognitive changes before consulting with the prescribing physician. Most medications prescribed are crucial to the treatment of a patient's medical problems, and changes in dose or kind of medication must be considered carefully. For most medical problems, however, there are alternative drugs that can be substituted for ones that may cause subtle adverse effects.

Physical, mental status, and neurological examinations will be supplemented with an electrocardiogram (EKG), blood and urine studies, and frequently a neuroimaging scan (CT, MRI, SPECT) of the brain. Written screening tests of cognitive function and depression may be given, as well as more detailed neuropsychiatric tests. Tests of hearing and vision should be made to be sure that the patient is performing maximally on the cognitive testing and also to ensure that some people with sensory impairments are not mistakenly diagnosed as being demented.

The medical, neurological, and psychiatric evaluations of the patient with dementia help to define the diagnosis, and if possible, what can be done to treat it. They also allow the physician to stage the disease in an effort to estimate the extent of the disability and the ways in which the patient might remain functional for a period of time. Although the course of any individual case of a dementing disorder is quite variable, an estimate can be made of what the patient and family members may expect in the near future. The medical and psychiatric assessment helps evaluate the patient's other medical and psychiatric problems and gives the physician baseline knowledge of the patient's health so that medications and other treatments can be given judiciously and the effects properly evaluated. The evaluation process also includes a caregiver—a family member and/or friend, if one is available, who will be directly or indirectly responsible for the patient's care over time. The caregiving role with patients who are demented is an extensive one, and the caregiver requires and deserves information, support, and guidance in his role. That all begins with the initial evaluation.

Alzheimer's Disease

Background

Alzheimer's disease is the disorder that most people think of in connection with dementia. It is not only the most publicly known dementing illness; it is the most heavily researched and clinically reported of the dementias.

Alzheimer's disease was first described by Dr. Alois Alzheimer, a psychiatrist, in 1907. His first case was a 51-year-old woman who presented with paranoid delusions and increasing memory problems. These symptoms progressed to global intellectual impairment, including inability to read, write, and remember names of common objects. For example, when stumped for a word, such as *cup*, the patient said "milk pourer." After four and one-half years of mental and physical deterioration, she died. On autopsy, Alzheimer identified tangles of nerve fibrils and plaques of material when the brain tissue was examined microscopically. These tangles and plaques were the hallmarks of this new disorder and remain an important postmortem finding, when this diagnosis is made.

From 1907 until the 1960s, Alzheimer's disease was regarded as a relatively rare presenile dementia, occurring in people under the age of 65. People over 65 years who were demented were referred to as *senile*. In the mid- to late 1960s several British and American scientists made the startling discoveries that the specific neuropathological changes identified sixty years earlier by Dr. Alzheimer as characteristically present in the brains of people with progressive presenile dementia were also present in the brains of many older people dying of "senility." In addition, the number of plaques and tangles in the brains, on postmortem examination, was correlated with the extent of the dementia. These discoveries dramatically changed the definition of Alzheimer's disease to include all patients having a characteristic course of progressive dementia, in the absence of other medical and psychological causes of dementia, and with the diagnostic plaques and tangles in the brain tissue on postmortem microscopic examination. The issue of age was moot. In fact, most of the cases of Alzheimer's disease are in people over the age of 65. By the early 1970s, Alzheimer's disease became the focus of increasing study and research as it was clear that the majority of patients previously considered to have had some nonspecific entity called senility, in fact, had a disorder called Alzheimer's disease.

The findings of the late 1960s and early 1970s brought a rapid expansion of interest in Alzheimer's disease, which continues today. Federal and private research grants increasingly support studies to define the cause of Alzheimer's disease, which is still unknown, to understand the specific pathological changes in the brains of people with Alzheimer's disease, to develop a specific diagnostic test that would help make the early diagnosis of Alzheimer's disease, and to discover definitive treatments. There has been new interest in the study of memory and intellectual functioning. There are continuing controversies about whether there is a continuum of memory failure with age or whether there are distinct categorical diagnoses of intellectual impairment at various points in middle and late life. There is still no definitive diagnostic test for Alzheimer's disease, the most common of the dementias, and no definitive or curative treatments.

Alzheimer's disease is a clinical diagnosis with specific criteria outlined in the DSM-IIIR of the American Psychiatric Association (and soon-to-be published DSM-IV). The NINCDS-ADRDA Work Group of the Department of Health and Human

Services Task Force on Alzheimer's Disease provided more specific criteria for the probable diagnosis of Alzheimer's disease.* Recently there has been increased speculation that Alzheimer's disease is a group of disorders that may have similar clinical findings but multiple, differing, or overlapping causes. In addition, there have been case reports in which the clinical presentation and course of the patient resembled that of Alzheimer's disease, and the postmortem autopsy findings showed atrophy in the areas of the brain that are most affected in Alzheimer's disease, but none or few of the classic plaques and tangles were present.

Neuroscience research has uncovered a number of changes in neurotransmitter and receptor function in normal aging adults and in patients with various of the dementias, principally Alzheimer's disease. These have led to exciting future prospects for diagnosis and treatment.† Studies indicate that brain size and brain weight are decreased, due to atrophy, in people with Alzheimer's disease when compared to normal people in their 60s. But when normal "old old" people are compared with Alzheimer's disease patients, the differences are harder to detect.

It is clear that in patients with Alzheimer's disease, there is a deficiency in the brain of a wide range of neurotransmitters, the brain chemicals that facilitate the functioning of the neuronal cells of the brain. Unlike the story of the treatment of Parkinson's disease, where L-dopa increases the production of the neurotransmitter dopamine necessary to correct at least some of the symptoms present, attempts to replace one or another of the neurotransmitters or their precursors, have not proved to be an answer to the mysteries of the origin of or potential treatment for Alzheimer's disease. University-based, government, and privately supported research scientists and pharmaceutical manu-

---

*McKhann D. Drachman, M. Folstein, "Clinical Diagnosis of Alzheimer's Disease: Report of the NINCDS-ADRDA Work Group under the Auspices of Department of Health and Human Services Task Force on Alzheimer's Disease," *Neurology*, 34:939–944, (1984).

†R. Katzman and J. E. Jackson, "Alzheimer disease: Basic and Clinical Advances," *Journal of the American Geriatrics Society* 39:516–525 (1991).

facturers are developing and testing a wide range of compounds and techniques for their administration, which might work to enhance or inhibit aspects of neurotransmission. Research has extended to medications used for other medical disorders that produce incidental neurotransmitter enhancement. Some of these are now being evaluated for possible roles in slowing the course or reversing the damage of Alzheimer's disease. There is also considerable interest in the role of genetics in Alzheimer's disease and of some specific chromosomal changes in particular. Amyloid, an abnormal protein found in the brains of people with Alzheimer's disease, is the subject of much study as to its roles as cause or effect in this disorder. Although the brain has been assumed not to have significant regeneration capacities, there is ongoing research in nerve growth factors that increase the branching capacity of neurons and the possibility that the brain does yet have some undifferentiated tissue that could serve as the basis for new neuron development, as occurs in some other organs of the body. These could yield major inroads in the search for significant treatments and cures.

The fact that Alzheimer's disease has become one of the "popular" diseases of the late twentieth century is caused by the increasingly large aging population, particularly the growth of "the old old" segment; the certainty that the incidence of Alzheimer's increases with age; the probability that this illness will have immense medical, social, financial, and public health consequences in the coming decades; the fact that the neurosciences are part of an area of medical science that is relatively new and rapidly advancing, with ramifications to various aspects of brain functioning and disease; and the development of an active and vocal advocacy and support network through the Alzheimer's Association. The danger in the popularity of this disease is that the general public, physicians, and mental health professionals will assume that all memory failure is due to Alzheimer's disease, and patients may not be adequately evaluated for the memory changes that might accompany normal aging and the many diagnoses that are not Alzheimer's disease but are identifiable and potentially treatable medical and psychiatric problems.

Alzheimer's disease now accounts for 50 to 60 percent of the cases of dementia, approximately 5 percent of the more than 32 million people over the age of 65, and at least 10 to 15 percent of the group over 75 years of age. Age is the greatest risk factor for having the disease, with only 1 percent of the population between 65 and 70 years afflicted but at least 25 percent, and possibly more, of the population over 85 years being diagnosed with Alzheimer's disease. If it were accurately reported on death certificates, Alzheimer's disease would be the fourth leading cause of death among older adults. Until a cause or causes can be determined and until definitive treatments can be instituted, it represents a catastrophic illness of great proportions.

The Quest for Causes of Alzheimer's Disease

The cause of Alzheimer's disease remains unknown, although several major areas of research are being pursued toward discovering causes and definitive treatments. Since it is possible, indeed probable, that Alzheimer's disease is more than one entity with similar clinical features or that there are several varieties or subtypes of one disorder with one or more causes of each, the pursuit of a number of causes is reasonable and is ongoing.

THE CHOLINERGIC HYPOTHESIS. Acetylcholine, one of the major neurotransmitters in the brain, has been the most studied of those vital brain chemicals for its role in Alzheimer's disease. There is evidence that acetylcholine is relatively decreased in the brains of patients with Alzheimer's disease. Certain areas of the brain, such as the hippocampus, that are normally rich in acetylcholine and are areas of production of the neurotransmitter are selectively damaged in these patients. Efforts to increase acetylcholine in the brain through different routes of administration and by altering various chemical pathways to the production of acetylcholine have thus far been unsuccessful in slowing or reversing the cognitive changes of the disease. There is an increasingly prevalent belief by research scientists in this field that Alzheimer's disease is most likely due to deficiencies or changes in more than one neurotransmitter, in fact to an array of brain chemicals including amino acids, neuropeptides, and others that are decreased in this disease and probably in some of the other dementias as well. This notion greatly complicates the search for a cure.

G E N E T I C O R I G I N S. Several researchers have pointed to the fact that, for at least a subset of cases, Alzheimer's disease arises out of a genetic predisposition. Studying the genetics of this disorder is complicated by the age-related incidence and the fact that some potential cases probably die of other diseases prior to advanced age, when the incidence of Alzheimer's disease would be highest. Some studies show that the risks to family members are higher if the identified patient is diagnosed at an early age (less than 70 years of age) rather than later.

Chromosome 21 is abnormal in patient's with Down's syndrome. In fact, the disorder results from an extra chromosome at that location. Virtually all patients with Down's syndrome who die in mid-life have changes of Alzheimer's disease in their brains, and this has spurred interest in the relationship between chromosome 21 and Alzheimer's disease. Chromosome 21 is also the location of the gene that is responsible for the production of beta-amyloid, an abnormal protein found in the characteristic neuritic plaques. Other chromosomal locations have been studied. Twin studies demonstrate that identical (monozygotic) twins do not have 100 percent concordance, indicating that factors other than genetics probably play key roles in the origins of this disease. For now, it appears that there is a genetic factor in some groups of cases of Alzheimer's disease, but the precise genetic mechanism and interaction with other factors are still unclear.

T O X I C C A U S E S. The role of aluminum as a toxic cause of Alzheimer's disease has been studied extensively and is of particular interest to research teams in the United Kingdom. Although aluminum is present in the senile plaques and neurofibrillary tangles of the Alzheimer's patients' brains and not in normal brain tissue, it is uncertain what role it plays, if any, in the disorder. Other metals and alcohol, capable of causing dementia in excessive amounts, have also been investigated for a possible role in Alzheimer's disease.

INFECTIOUS AGENTS. Because of the similarities between Alzheimer's disease and Jakob-Creutzfeldt disease, a rare dementing disorder caused by an infectious agent, there has been speculation that viruses similar to ones that cause Jakob-Creutzfeldt may be responsible for Alzheimer's as well. To date, there is no evidence of a specific infectious agent as a cause for Alzheimer's disease.

HEAD INJURY. There are studies that show a higher rate of head injury in the past histories of patients with Alzheimer's disease than in the general population. No explanation for the role of head injury has been postulated, nor does it explain the vast majority of cases of Alzheimer's disease.

ABNORMAL PROTEINS. Amyloid is an abnormal protein found in the plaques of patients with Alzheimer's disease. It is unclear whether it is a cause or an effect of the disorder. Amyloid and its precursor protein are the subject of intense study by molecular biologists who see them as potential links to the understanding of the early development of Alzheimer's disease. Understanding the role of abnormal proteins found in the brains of patients with Alzheimer's disease may yield an essential piece of the puzzle of causation and also lead to a means of definitive identification of patients with the disorder. The tau protein is another abnormal substance that has been found in the neurofibrillary tangles in the brains of people with Alzheimer's disease.

Course of the Disease

Typically, Alzheimer's disease begins insidiously. As in the case of Mr. M., cited above, by the time patients and their families approach a clinician about a suspected dementia problem, there have been subtle signs and symptoms for a year or two. The patient may initially appear to be having some normal-for-age changes in memory, forgetting names of familiar people or the names of common objects around the house. But unlike most other normally aging people, this person cannot retrieve the words easily or remember them again after a period of time or after being helped to remember them. This forgetting progresses so that work or hobbies become difficult to perform, particularly when new information must be integrated. The patient may appear entirely "normal" to the outside world; only in retrospect will this period be recognized as the earliest point in the disorder. These lapses result in anxiety and depressive symptoms because the patient begins to notice that he or she is "slipping"; those symptoms tend to exaggerate the memory impairment and functional disability.

Alzheimer's disease is variable in terms of the progression of a person's overall ability to function at usual activities and the extent to which specific symptoms appear to worsen. There are patients who deteriorate at a rapid rate and go from being fairly well functioning to quite vegetative in a year's time, while others seem to reach a plateau of functioning and remain there for months to several years. Most people deteriorate across the whole spectrum of cognitive skills, but some retain function in one or more areas while having lost almost all other skills. One man no longer knew his own name or that of his wife, but he remembered the names of several companies of which he owned shares of stock, and each morning he searched the business section of the newspaper for more than an hour, looking for changes in their worth. Another man was equally disabled but remembered his daughter's birthday at a stage when he was otherwise virtually nonverbal. The average survival from time of diagnosis is between seven and ten years. Over the months and years, the patient is progressively less able to function in the areas of memory (recent and remote), orientation, concentration, ability to integrate new information, judgment, activities of daily living, and behavioral stability. Between one-third and one-half of the patients develop psychotic symptoms, including delusions and hallucinations, particularly late in the disease. Approximately one-third are significantly depressed, typically early in the course of the illness.

Although there is some controversy about whether dementia proceeds in a set pattern of symptoms, over the years there is usually a progression that can be described as early, middle, and late stages, with representative sets of symptoms at each stage. There is considerable variability in timing and in symptom occurrence in any one individual.

In the early stage of dementia there is a small but definite progression from the subtle memory changes that affected individuals may alone notice. There is noticeable forgetfulness; individuals may increasingly misplace things, have word-finding problems, repeat themselves, and lose interest in usual activities. They may be anxious, withdrawn, apathetic, and depressed. They realize that something "bad" is happening. While the specific changes at this stage may be noticed only by those affected and family members and close friends, it may be apparent to others that something is wrong. Patients at this point generally remain oriented to person (identifying themselves and the people around them), place (knowing where they are), and time (knowing the day, date, season, time of day), although they may have trouble following directions and they get lost in unfamiliar places. There is little disruption in their ability to perform activities of daily and self-care.

In the middle stage, memory problems increase. There is poor knowledge of recent family events and details of past history, which were formerly well known to the person and are now forgotten or, at least, very blurry. The ability to concentrate is clearly decreased, with markedly diminished attention span, except to a rare activity. There are mistakes in orientation and difficulty handling money and other complex tasks, including work situations that are not highly routinized. During this time, there are wider gaps in vocabulary, with a considerable amount of repetitiveness or decreased verbalization. It is difficult for patients to understand everything said to them, although they may not seek clarification. Although most basic activities of daily living are intact, the patient may need assistance in grooming, bathing, choosing clothes, and using kitchen utensils. This is a time when there may be considerable apathy and withdrawal or irritability and agitation. Agitation may take the form of wandering, pacing, shouting, striking out, and other behaviors (discussed more fully later in the chapter). Sleep disturbances are common, with shifts to earlier bedtimes or midnight awakenings. Wandering about the house or even attempts to leave the house may occur. Hallucinations and delusions may be present during this phase.

In the late stage of dementia, those affected are very confused. They cannot concentrate, even to count to ten; they are completely unaware of recent and past experiences, may not know the names of spouse or children, or even their own; do not know the year; have decreasing speech to a point of total aphasia; cannot perform most activities of daily living, including dressing, toileting, and eating without assistance, and at some point develop incontinence—first urinary, then fecal. The patient may be grossly agitated, and up to one-third of patients have hallucinations and delusions. In this stage, patients are eventually bedridden and require full nursing care because the neuronal death involves areas of the brain cortex that control walking, talking, swallowing, and other motor functions. Sometimes there are episodes of aspiration (choking) on food because of the deteriorated muscular/nervous control of the swallowing mechanism. Death resulting from Alzheimer's disease comes about in several ways, most often from pneumonia or other infections, dehydration, malnutrition, and general wasting. Some older patients who have Alzheimer's disease or other dementias over many years die of intercurrent heart attacks, cancer, or strokes unrelated to their being demented, although patients with Alzheimer's disease are usually otherwise relatively healthy.

Several Alzheimer's disease researchers have described more elaborate staging schemes useful in clinical research to track patterns of symptom development and to attempt to predict the course of the illness more precisely. The Global Deterioration

Scale (GDS), devised by Reisberg and his colleagues, is an example of a detailed instrument for grading the extent of deterioration of cognitive function. In the evaluation and continuing care by a clinician, scales such as the GDS will likely be used with other assessments and psychiatric evaluations, to follow the pattern of the individual's course.*

Pharmacological Treatment of Dementia

There is no cure or definitive treatment for most forms of dementia, but there have been numerous attempts to discover effective treatments. Although all the dementias result in a panoply of behavioral and affective symptoms, the primary and most disabling problem is that of progressive cognitive impairment. There is great interest in the search for a cure for that basic aspect of the disorder; a significant reversal or slowing of dementing symptoms might make the difference, in groups of patients, between functional existence in the community and institutional care, between a normal or near-normal old age in a supportive family setting and the ravages of cognitive decline.

Attempts to find pharmacological agents that might be effective treatments are complicated by confounding factors in the older population, such as multiple medical illnesses, multiple medications, the variability inherent in normal aging and in the symptoms and rate of change of patients with some form of dementia, and the likelihood that even the single entity of Alzheimer's disease is a many-faceted disorder, with perhaps multiple and overlapping causes. Nonetheless, following on the increasing evidence that changes in several neurotransmitters are probably involved in the deficits of Alzheimer's disease and perhaps other dementias, there has been considerable interest in medications that might substantially increase the availability of

*B. Reisberg, S.H. Ferris, M.J. de Leon, and T. Crook, "The Global Deterioration Scale for Assessment of Primary Degenerative Dementia," *American Journal of Psychiatry* 139:1136–1139 (1982).

those essential brain chemicals to the synapse junctions between nerve cells.*

Although the role of the neurotransmitter, acetylcholine, was implicated in dementia prior to 1986, the publication of an article in that year sparked interest in tetrahydroaminoacridine (THA), the drug used by Summers and his colleagues that reportedly resulted in significant cognitive improvement in patients with Alzheimer's disease.† The study was methodologically flawed in several respects, but it nonetheless began an era of intense research into drugs, like THA, that increase cholinergic activity at the synapses of neurons. A multicenter study was begun in the United States to assess, under rigorous standards, the effectiveness of THA. The results were largely inconclusive, with some patients benefiting and others not; the rate of side effects was substantial. This study and others have stimulated interest in compounds related to THA and other neurotransmitter enhancers, which continue to be tested by pharmaceutical manufacturers and other research teams, as do other agents that enhance other neurotransmitter functioning. It is likely that the compounds under current consideration will be the first or second generation in a line of medications that will possibly be refined to produce an increasingly effective medication with fewer adverse effects.

In view of the idea that Alzheimer's disease is probably a disorder that involves multiple factors in neurotransmission, a wide range of novel medications, and some already in use for other medical indications, are in the process of being tested for effectiveness in slowing or reversing cognitive impairment. Agents that change the availability of serotonin, glutamate, and neuropeptides, such as somatostatin, corticotrophin releasing factor, and neurotrophic growth factor, are being studied. Antihyper-

---

*L.J. Whalley, "Drug Treatment of Dementia," *British Journal of Psychiatry* 155 (1989):595–611.

†W.K. Summers, L.V. Majovski, G.M. March, *et al.*, "Oral Tetrahydroaminoacridine in Long-term Treatment of Senile Dementia, Alzheimer's Type," *New England Journal of Medicine* 315:1241–1245 (1986).

tensive medications, including calcium channel blocking agents and ACE inhibitors, may have a potential role in treating dementias of vascular origin but also are being investigated for effectiveness in other dementias.

So-called nootropic agents that generally enhance brain activity have been marketed and used for the treatment of Alzheimer's disease in the United States and Europe. They are thought to work as nonspecific enhancers of neuronal metabolism. Dihydroergotamine mesylate (Hydergine) has some positive effects as a nonspecific agent in some individual patients in the early stages of the disease, but evidence is lacking for significant cognitive improvement as a result of treatment with it. It may have some stimulating effect, so patients (and therefore family members) feel better for a time.

To date there are no strong candidates for the effective treatment of the cognitive impairment of the dementias, but neuroscience has advanced more in the last decade than in all the years prior to that. There is cause to be optimistic that within the next two decades a definitive treatment will be discovered.

Techniques to Assist Cognitive Functioning

Certainly in the earlier stages of dementia, having some techniques for dealing with declining memory and other cognitive functions is useful. Often patients on their own develop some methods of remembering.

> Mr. T., a patient of mine with Alzheimer's disease, was an expert amateur automobile mechanic. As his cognitive skills declined, he began to make reminder notes in the owner's manual that came with his car, something he never needed to do during his healthier years. Later, one of his son's found the manual filled with rather basic instructions Mr. T. had made for himself. Although he was probably embarrassed and frightened during that period, Mr. T. may have extended the time over which he was able to work on his car, and, using

similar methods, in other ways creatively maintained his functioning, albeit with some limitations.

The caregiver and the patient may be able to work on some basic aids to assist in remembering certain things around the house and in other familiar environments. Having a large bulletin board in a prominent location can be helpful. It can list important telephone numbers, names and pictures of close relatives, a schedule for the day, and a place for memos about who visited or called on the telephone or where a member of the household has gone. Reminders to go to the bathroom, turn off the stove, and eat lunch can be followed by the patient who is left alone for periods of time, in the early stages. These should always be placed in the same "memo" area so the patient has little difficulty locating them.

A variety of high-tech devices have been invented for use by chronically ill people and those with various disabilities, and some corporations specialize in marketing these. Special telephones can be programmed so that photographs can be placed in such a way that pressing a photograph of the person to be called dials the number of that person. In the early stages of dementia, when the patient is left alone or with a companion, having such a device can be reassuring. Having calendars and clocks with large numbers in prominent locations is important. The caregiver should draw attention to them daily when talking about the schedule. Labeling important locations in the house with a word or picture is useful. The locations of the patient's room, bathroom, living area, and the contents of cupboards and drawers are some of the places that get confusing to the patient with dementia. At night, when the patient may get more disoriented, even at home, having a well-lit path to the bathroom and to a room where the patient may sit is crucial. Maintaining the house decor the same, the furniture in place, and the environment as stable as possible is reassuring to the patient.

An environment in which stress is minimized probably affords the patient with dementia the best opportunity to function maximally. Tailoring social situations, outings, visits, and entertainment activities for the patient is important. For most demented patients, having stimulation of various kinds is enjoyable; for some, it is taxing and anxiety provoking and may precipitate a period of agitation. Activity has to be structured and modulated to suit the needs of the individual. If the event is to involve people that the patient should know, rehearsing the names of those people using photographs or flash cards may be helpful. Mr. T. would rehearse my name with his wife prior to visits with me because, even into the middle stage of the disease, it was important to him to be able to greet me properly and for him not to be embarrassed by his declining cognitive function.

Activities that the patient formerly enjoyed should be continued as long as possible. Listening to the radio and watching television, particularly news programs, may serve some reorientation purposes, and other programs assist with relaxation and fun. Playing a musical instrument should be encouraged if it was a part of the patient's life in healthier days. Dancing, doing artwork and household chores, and reading the newspaper are all possible, depending on the individual patient's desires and capabilities at the time and the availability of proper supervision. Mr. T. greatly enjoyed playing the piano and dancing to radio music well into the middle stage of the disorder. His family reported that he "seemed to be transported into a special feeling state" when he played the piano or danced. Some people enjoy being read to by caregivers; others listen to stories or music on tape, using a small cassette player and earphones, which the patient can control. Throughout this debilitating disease, efforts are made to maintain as much function and enjoyment as possible, while trying not to frustrate, belittle, or stress the patient. Most caregivers, particularly those who know, or get to know, the patient well, develop a sense of this balance.

Finally, it is vital to talk and to touch. Although they have diminished functional ability in many respects, patients with Alzheimer's disease very much demonstrate the strength of their lifelines of relationships, experiences, and inherent personality attributes. These assets are part of who they are as people; caregivers, other family members, and clinicians who work with them should remember the value of those lifelines, even in an increasingly disabled person, and reinforce them for their positive value. Most people with early Alzheimer's disease remember their earlier days better than the recent, and reminiscing with them about relationships and experiences can be supportive, enlightening, and fun for both the participants. As long as the person can talk, feelings can be expressed, desires stated, and a sense of relationship maintained through talk. Their past relationships, experiences, and personality characteristics are evident in their conversation, particularly in the early and middle stages. Mr. T.'s history of strong and close relationships with friends and family was sustaining to him and his wife throughout the disease. I will never forget his determination to remember, to do well on tests of cognitive function, and his great pride in whatever he did. These attributes were part of him in health and disease.

Sometimes later in the diseases, thoughts and words become a bit confused, and the caregiver needs to make special efforts to understand the patient. The conversations are worth pursuing. When cognitive faculties fail, it is even more important to get other inputs. Communications through facial expressions, body movements, and physical contact continue well into the disease. Touching as part of the caring activities, holding hands, kissing (if appropriate), massaging, and other forms of touch maintain the relationship and are reassuring, calming, and caring long after verbal communication is deteriorated. Mr. T., unable to speak but a few words and showing little overt recognition of whom his wife was, would hold tight to her hand when they sat on the living room couch. That was soothing to him, and for her, for many months.

Special Problems in Patient Care

The diagnosis of Alzheimer's disease is a catastrophic one. The disorder progresses in an inexorable pattern toward death, although there can be years of adequate functioning and near-normal life between the time of diagnosis and a time of significant deterioration. The simple functions of everyday life change dramatically for the person with Alzheimer's disease, the caregivers within the family, and even for the more distant relatives and friends. There are the more pronounced difficulties of behavioral changes, total loss of memory, social ramifications, financial burdens, personal and marital stress, schedules and places for care, and more.

The starting point is dealing with the fact of the diagnosis. For some patients and family members, having the diagnosis of Alzheimer's disease made by a competent clinician is a relief. They have known that something was wrong, have used much energy trying to cover up or deny and trying not to be too sad, frightened, and angry. By the time they hear the diagnosis, people who do not extensively use denial usually know the situation. They may have been to several or more doctors, clinics, and specialists and are weary of that process. The ways in which patients and families cope with the diagnosis and its aftermath is as variable as the nature of the disease itself. "The diagnosis is made; now we can deal with it," one patient's wife declared, while another took more than a month to take some initial steps to tell her adult children and to contact the local Alzheimer's Association for the support she greatly needed. Patients, families, and other caregivers will cope with the information imparted much as they have dealt with other crises. The clinicians involved should respect those styles but also guide the patient and caregiver to obtain the continuing assistance they will need.

Dealing with Friends and Family

Telling others about Alzheimer's disease can be difficult. Because it is an incurable illness of the brain, many people still view the disease as a mental illness, as a mysterious illness, or as something to do with syphilis. They see the patient as "crazy," potentially out of control, and primitive, and all that is frightening to them. Most patients with Alzheimer's disease do not act crazy or out of control. The disease is not contagious. Most frightening to people who hear about it is that it can happen to anyone regardless of socioeconomic status, education, general health and fitness, moral character, and any other factors, as far as we know. We do not know what underlying characteristics distinguish people who get Alzheimer's disease from those who do not. That reality can be difficult to face. These are important areas of research, but the uncertainties are frightening to those we must tell, and many of them would rather keep their distance. Others keep their distance because they do not know how to be with someone whom they used to know as cognitively intact and who is now impaired, or they are embarrassed, sad, or grieving. Still others are reminded of the "senility" that their own parents, spouse, or other relatives suffered, and living it again with a friend is too uncomfortable for them. That is an unfortunate reaction for those who have Alzheimer's disease and for the family and friends who care for them and, ultimately, for those who create the distance. Patients and families need friends and relatives for support, both for practical aspects of daily life like helping with doctors' appointments and picking up groceries at the store, and for emotional support, when a shoulder is needed for tears, when a caregiver needs to tell someone how frustrated and angry he or she is, when a patient needs the smile of a familiar face as a reminder of the past smiles, and so many other things that one can use when trying to cope with an all-consuming catastrophic illness.

Telling people about a loved one with Alzheimer's disease is best done in a straightforward way. It may be helpful to try to educate them if they are not already educated about dementia and what it can do to a patient and his family. If they are interested, there are several good books on the subject. *The 36-Hour Day* is one of the best guides for families coping with Alzheimer's disease.* Caregivers can tell others what they may need from them, how they can be helpful, how the patient has changed, and what his or her limitations are. Sometimes friends

*N.L. Mace and P.V. Rabins, *The 36-Hour Day* (Baltimore: Johns Hopkins University Press, 1991).

and family need support while they get used to the fact that Jim or Mary cannot participate, as well or at all, in conversation. Families initially pull together or do not; if they do not, they may be helped by a family physician or mental health professional to do so. Ultimately a spouse or a child or both bear the responsibility for caregiving or for organizing it and hiring others to do the day-to-day care. Families that are cohesive can offer much love, caring, and support to the patient and primary caregiver. For family members in conflict, a catastrophic illness can be even more than devastating. I am reminded again of the T. family, which joined forces to take charge of the situation in a positive way.

> I diagnosed Mr. T. as having dementia, probably Alzheimer's disease, and told the family about it in a family meeting in which Mr. and Mrs. T. and their three sons and their spouses participated. It was clear that Mrs. T. would take care of her husband on a day-to-day basis, and she had already begun the process of finding out about a local support group. In the family meeting, the concern and devotion of the sons and daughters-in-law was apparent in their words and body language from the start. Although several had difficulty seeing their father deteriorate, each participated in his care and that of their mother. One son spent an evening and part of a weekend day with his father, while his mother relaxed or did errands. Another telephoned every day and spoke to both his father and mother, stopping by occasionally in the evening on the way home from work. The third who lived in another city, telephoned regularly and about once per month visited for a weekend. The two daughters-in-law in the area either took their mother-in-law out to the theater or movie, or shopping or to church, at least weekly, while another stayed with Mr. T. A neighbor and close friend accompanied Mr. and Mrs. T. on every doctor visit in case there was need for additional assistance. Although Mrs. T. was entirely competent and probably tended to be too self-denying, the real and emotional involvement that both she and her husband had with family and friends made the early and middle stages of the disorder easier to handle. When they decided that Mrs. T.

could no longer care for him at home, and it was best that he go into a long-term-care facility, it was a combined family decision, with all recognizing that this signaled the beginning of the end and supporting each other in the process.

Periodic family meetings give support to the primary caregiver and patient and allow the others in the family to get a progress report, to see where they may help, and to encourage the primary person to have assistance so that she or he can live at least some aspects of life normally. The family meetings help to minimize fantasies about the situation and allow some of the difficult realities to be shared among the available people. How is everybody doing? Is Mom or Dad or sister (the caregiver) getting regular respite from caring? Are there difficulties with the children and adolescents? What do they think about what is happening to Grandpa? They should have their own opportunities to talk with a knowledgeable adult and to clarify misconceptions.

One friend of mine carried index cards in his pocket that said, "Please excuse my wife's behavior. She may not communicate as easily as she used to; she has Alzheimer's disease." When they met someone in church or while shopping who looked surprised to see his wife, my friend would hand out a card. He felt that people could deal with the information in their individual ways. He commented, "At times like this, you learn how flexible people are. You learn not so much about who your friends are but more about what your friends are! Some people just can't manage to be supportive either because their lives are so chaotic or because yours is so scary to them."

Caregiver Feelings

The primary caregiver is usually a spouse or adult child, often a daughter or daughter-in-law, a hired companion, or nursing assistant or some combination of these.* The primary person may

*E. M. Brody *Women in the Middle: Their Parent-Care Years* (New York: Springer Publishing Co., 1990).

be the actual day-to-day provider of care or may orchestrate the care, being ultimately responsible that it works. The day-to-day work of caregiving is exhausting, frustrating, stressful, and saddening. It totally occupies the lives of the caregivers, emotionally and physically. It can be satisfying and even exhilarating. It can be part of a natural continuum of caring by a spouse for a mate, and it can renew or reinforce a parent-child relationship, with the child feeling needed in the parent's time of distress.

> Mr. G., a 72-year-old man who retired at age 65 to take care of his wife with Alzheimer's disease, said, "I've loved her for more than forty years; I didn't stop loving her because she had dementia. I thought it was an act of continuing love to take care of her. Who would do a better job anyway?" This unusual man worked out a plan where in the early stages of the disease he cared for her at home alone. Gradually, as she became more demanding, he brought in a nursing assistant to help him, and after three years, he enrolled her in an adult day center for people with dementia. By the fifth year, his wife was too demented to participate in the day center. He found a "foster home" for her, which was run by a young couple who cared for several residents with dementia. She stayed there on the weekdays and returned home to her husband on the weekends. Mr. G. talked to his wife constantly, not knowing how much she really understood. She had always loved to sing, and she did remember the words of childhood songs and hymns well into her illness, when most other memories were gone. With a flexible approach to care, this family worked out a system that allowed maximum contact with spouse and family, while minimizing burden. They were also lucky. Mr. G. was healthy and hearty, they could afford the auxiliary care, and they found a foster home situation that provided consistent and attentive care to their residents.

Mr. G. had difficulty expressing his negative feelings about difficult aspects of life, and the years of care of his wife were no exception. He focused instead on what she could still do at various points in the illness: do needlework, remember and sing songs, and give him hugs. Toward the end, when she was non-verbal, emaciated, incontinent, and agitated, it was difficult for him to let go. Mrs. G. died of Alzheimer's disease and pneumonia. Mr. G. mourned her loss, felt proud of the care he had given her, and gradually recovered by volunteering to help other families learn to cope with their chronically ill family members.

As a result of Alzheimer's disease or others of the dementias, spouses, children, and grandchildren gradually lose their relationships with an important member of the family. The spouse loses a companion, although he or she is still alive, and the children lose the parent, friend, guide, and teacher, who was very different in the past. The grieving inherent in these losses often is not openly discussed enough but remains a major psychological stress with which the family and friends must cope.

Many caregivers do not realize how difficult the task is and will become. They have trouble dealing with their anger and subsequent guilt. They work hard to take care of their loved one but resent the fact that they are caretakers to an invalid. This can be true of spouses who hoped for years of relative ease in retirement and younger people, who have their own marriages to worry about and their own children for whom to care. Those people need help to continue in their caregiving role or to give it up to an employed attendant or to an institution, such as an assisted-living residence or nursing home. It is not realistic for all family members to take on the roles of primary caregivers and do it successfully. Some people find this out early in the effort, and others burn out along the way. They can be helped to see this as other than an all-or-nothing venture. Their relative with dementia may do better with auxiliary or residential care, having the family able to give what they can emotionally and practically, than to have the spouse or children angry, exhausted, bitter, and ultimately giving little to the patient's needs. Family members can work through their role with the help of an understanding physician or mental health professional, so that the best possible care plan is tailored to consider patient needs, family strengths, capabilities and desires, finances, housing, and other practical issues. Most families struggle with the issues of care of their loved ones. It is almost always a wrenching experience, inducing a mixture of feelings that include profound sadness, anger, guilt, and fear about what will ultimately happen to the patient and what will happen to those who survive.

Caregiver Burden and Stress

Caregivers of patients with Alzheimer's disease are susceptible to depression, anxiety, fatigue, hypertension, peptic ulcer disease, and other stress-related disorders, at a higher rate than in the general public. Caregiving produces stress and burden and their consequences, whether one is actually taking care of a patient or supervising or monitoring the care of a family member performed by someone else. The care and health of the primary caregiver is often overlooked, and yet it is essential, if the system or plan of care is to be effective, that the caregiver do all that is possible to maintain health and prevent illness. The job of caregiving does not allow much time or energy for oneself, and yet that time must be scheduled, even if it means asking friends and relatives to assist with care or hiring a companion or assistant for several hours of the week to make the plan work. While the patient and caregiver may be able to enjoy some activities together, the caregiver needs time away from these intensive responsibilities. Some social events, exercise, shopping, errands, and chores can be joint activities, although the caregiver will have to be vigilant to assess which activities are or become too stressful as the disease progresses and then take measures to modify them. The caregiver and the patient are in danger of being in relative isolation as friends and family flee from them. The caregiver must pursue others to continue to socialize appropriately.

Caregivers should focus on getting enough rest and sleep; eating a regular diet, with regular mealtimes; getting daily exercise, not only for its physical benefits but also for its role as an emotional release; continuing some regular social life; and regularly talking to people other than the patient. Stress management and relaxation techniques can be learned and should be regularly practiced. Participation in support groups organized by the Alzheimer's Association, and other agencies is an invaluable aid to every caregiver, even the most sophisticated and knowledgeable. Sometimes group or individual psychotherapy is needed to deal with the confusing multiple feelings and conflicts that caring for a spouse or parent presents. Caregivers often get so consumed with their caring duties that they forget that they need regular physical examinations and visits to their physician for care of their own medical problems and for prevention of new ones.

Management of Dementia

For most people with Alzheimer's disease, symptoms start slowly and progress over a period of one to two years before there is significant disability resulting from cognitive impairment. During this time, the patient is aware of changes in self, and close family members notice the early signs and symptoms. Although there is no cure for most people with dementia, early attention and diagnosis clarify the possibility of one of the reversible forms of dementia, which can then be effectively treated.

The progression of Alzheimer's disease and some other dementias is variable in speed and in the nature of the presenting symptoms. Sometimes the course is slow, and the patient enjoys a near-normal family and social life for several or more years, with few extreme symptoms. At other times, the course of the disorder is more turbulent, with agitation, insomnia, incontinence, inappropriate behaviors, and psychosis, in addition to the ubiquitous memory impairment and its consequences. Although the memory dysfunction is basic to the dementing disorders, the secondary symptoms are often the most troublesome for caregivers as they struggle to maintain their relatives and friends in the family home and in other community settings. The care of the demented patient is always difficult and exhausting for those who do it and for those who are concerned about the increasingly disabled patient. The task of physicians and mental health, nursing, and social work professionals who work with families and patients such as these is to help maximize the existing functioning, treat symptoms that interfere with functioning, and support the patient, caregivers, and other family members through the catastrophic illness.

A G I T A T I O N. *Agitation* is used commonly to mean "excitable, distractable, confused, fitful, and rambling." In describing demented patients as agitated, we mean all of those and more. Jiska Cohen-Mansfield and her associates at the Research Institute of the Hebrew Home of Greater Washington, D.C., has pioneered in the study of the behavioral aspects of agitation, particularly in patients with Alzheimer's disease, in both nursing home settings and other environments.* They define agitation as inappropriate verbal, vocal, or motor activity that is not an obvious expression of needs or confusion. Because of the nature of Alzheimer's disease and other dementias, it is possible that an individual's agitation is, in fact, an expression of a need or thought, but those are not apparent to the observer and not communicable by the patient or understandable by the caregiver. It is therefore crucial that every patient with agitation as a significant symptom be evaluated for possible medical, psychological, and environmental causes. For example, a patient may be disrobing at an inappropriate time or place because of a recent weight gain, so clothing is too tight. The patient may have no other mechanism for communicating that problem. A demented patient may be screaming because of pain or overturning a food tray repetitively and yelling, "shit, shit, shit," because he or she does not like the food being served. The awkward and primitive expressions may be the best the patient can do.

Agitated behaviors that are common at various stages of dementia include wandering, pacing, inappropriate disrobing, screaming, repetitive talking, hitting, and kicking. Although there are strong correlations between physical forms of agitation and cognitive impairment, that is not necessarily the case in other forms of agitation. Since agitation of all kinds is one of the

*J. Cohen-Mansfield, "Agitation in the Elderly", in N. Billig and P. V. Rabins, eds., *Issues in Geriatric Psychiatry: Advances in Psychosomatic Medicine* (Basel: Karger, 1989).

most upsetting symptoms with which caregivers must deal and because in nursing homes it consumes much staff time and energy, agitation is increasingly being studied for its specific relationships to dementia staging, premorbid patient personality, history and life-style characteristics, communication patterns, medical and psychological disorders, medications, and environmental issues. In its severe forms, agitation is one of the symptoms that most frequently results in families' having difficulty effectively managing demented patients at home. Another area of great interest to clinical researchers concerns possible treatment approaches that can be used to manage and/or prevent agitated behavior.

By far the most common treatment methods used to treat agitation are pharmacological. Before any symptomatic treatments are instituted, a thorough examination of possible correctable causes of agitation should be made. Attempting to discern whether the agitated behaviors represent covert messages of dissatisfaction, annoyance, distress, pain, illness, or environmental stress from the patient is vital to the patient's welfare. Neuroleptics (haloperidol, thioridazine, molindone, thiothixene) and benzodiazepines (lorazepam, alprazolam, clonazepam) are the most common classes of medications used to treat the various symptoms of agitation. The former are used more commonly when the patients are moderately to severely demented, sometimes also having hallucinations and delusions, and the latter more for mild or early stages of dementia. Antidepressant medications, beta-adrenergic blocking agents (propranolol), mood stabilizers (lithium, carbamazepine), and others have also been used to attempt to treat aspects of agitation. No one medication has emerged as the best or most effective in any clinical studies that have been performed. Many of these are effective in various situations, and all have adverse effects, which must be considered in their use. At times, medications might increase a patient's agitation, even after a time that it has been an effective treatment. Medications for agitation should be used sparingly, in the smallest possible doses. They should be regularly reevaluated and drug holidays (withdrawal) attempted periodically. The search for better medications for the treatment of agitation is being actively explored.

There are behavioral, environmental, and activity-oriented alternatives or adjuncts to the pharmacological treatment of agitation. Many of the behavioral schemes are based on reward or punishment paradigms, such as positive reinforcement for appropriate behaviors and restriction or distractive techniques for inappropriate agitated behaviors. Environmental approaches include increased staffing for more personal patient contact; the availability of large, safe, and secured indoor and outdoor areas for roaming and wandering; patient identification bracelets and bracelet alarms, so that patients can have wider access to spaces within a home, institution, or their confined surroundings; and visual cues near exits and locked doors to teach patients that they are not for their use.

The use of physical restraints, including bed rails, has come under increasing scrutiny in the United States, where they have, until recently, been used extensively in institutional and other settings, to safeguard agitated patients. With the examples of long-term-care settings in Scandinavia and the United Kingdom, there is now a strong movement to "untie the patient" and use more humane forms of treatment. There is no evidence that physical restraints increase the safety for even the most demented and agitated patients. In fact, they may increase the risk of certain dangers, such as falls out of bed, caused by patients' climbing over bed rails. The use of familiar furniture, pictures, and memorabilia in patient rooms has been tried in some settings, as has the availability of rocking and overstuffed chairs and pillows, which may be inviting and soothing for the agitated person.

Activities—music, dance, games, exercise, reality orientation, and art programs—have been found to be helpful in working with agitated demented people. Arts for the Aged, an innovative program begun in the Washington, D.C. area, trains professional artists and sponsors art classes in senior day centers, assisted-care residences, and long-term-care facilities. These effective structured arts activities include reminiscence techniques and artistic expression of feelings, thoughts, and memories.

Agitation is a complex set of symptoms, seen in most demented patients at some point in their illness, probably determined by a mixture of physical, psychological, and environmental factors. The research and clinical study of agitation has been ongoing only in the last decade and promises to bring new insights to bear on causation and management. Each person with dementia who exhibits signs of agitation should be examined for medical, psychiatric, and environmental causes, and treatment should be individualized to the extent possible, within the confines of the home or institutional environment. Rarely, an agitated demented patient will require hospitalization for monitoring of extreme symptoms and changes in complex medication regimens.

DEPRESSION. The dementia secondarily produced by a major depression has been discussed. Conversely, approximately 25 percent of the people who are primarily demented because of Alzheimer's disease and other disorders become significantly depressed. Early in the course of the illness, it is most likely due to the realization or news of a catastrophic diagnosis in which one's brain is progressively deteriorating. While that is something about which one should be sad, and even depressed, most people with the diagnosis of dementia are not depressed. Many people seem to cope with the diagnosis with considerable apathy or lack of awareness, although they may become anxious and agitated. Later in the course of the illness, depression, often difficult to diagnosis because of the severity of the dementia, is most likely due to the organic changes in the brain that affect neurotransmitter function. In either case, patients who are depressed as a complication of dementia respond to treatment with antidepressant medications. They may become less depressed and seem less cognitively impaired as the excess disability caused by the depression is lifted. Early in the dementia, while there are sufficient cognitive skills, some patients benefit from supportive psychotherapy, which helps them cope better with remaining functional capacity and deal with feelings of anger, fear, loss, and instability, which are part of any chronic deteriorative illness, especially this one. They may better understand with which activities and people they do best and how they can modify their lives to enjoy maximal functioning.

SLEEP DISTURBANCES. Sleep is frequently disturbed in patients with dementia because of the organic effects on the brain and because of the changes in life-style consequent to the disease. A restless or waking patient also brings a less than restful night's sleep for the caregiver. Some patients, probably because of the changes in the brain caused by the disease, have a changed sleep-wake cycle. The cycle may be advanced (early to bed) or delayed, with consequent disharmony with the way most other people are functioning. Some caregivers adjust their patterns to that of the patient, while others, with their physician's help, try various behavioral techniques or sedative/hypnotic or tranquilizing medications to assist the patient in having a more normal sleep-wake cycle. (See chapters 4 and 9.) Other sleep disorders, such as sleep apnea, may increase in severity and frequency in older and in demented patients.

Patients with dementia may awaken during the night because of frightening dreams, because they are restless, or to urinate. That may set off a cycle of disorientation, wandering around the house, and subsequent agitation. Having a small light or night light on near the patient and the bathroom is helpful for quick reorientation. Having the house doors, windows, appliances, and stairways secure for the night will prevent dangerous accidents. If the caregiver is awakened, he or she should try to be supportive and reassuring (sometimes difficult to do) and remind the patient to try to get back to sleep if it is still too early to awaken for the day. The patient and/or caregiver may develop a routine that allows the patient to return to sleep—turning on music, moving to another bed, having something to eat or drink.

Assuring that the bed, sleeping apparel, and environment are comfortable and attending to some of the basic sleep hygiene issues discussed in chapter 4 should also be done. Of particular importance is maintaining an exercise and activity program during the day, preventing daytime napping, monitoring fluid intake late in the day, and limiting caffeine-containing beverages and foods. Painful conditions, periodic leg movements, and urinary tract infections that might interfere with sleep should be treated. Medications of all sorts should be evaluated for their potential in causing either excessive sleepiness or stimulation. As a last resort, medications may be used to sedate the patient so both patient and caregiver can get sufficient rest. Chloral hydrate or relatively short-acting benzodiazepines can be used. If there is evidence of depression or sleep apnea, a sedating antidepressant might be helpful.

I N C O N T I N E N C E. Like agitation, incontinence is one of the symptoms that results in so much frustration that the family may feel forced to seek an institutional living situation for the demented patient. Although it is seen by many as an insurmountable problem, urinary incontinence is often correctable, or at least manageable, and many caregivers cope with it without difficulty. It may occur in the course of moderate to severe dementia, may be caused by urinary tract and pelvic abnormalities (prostate enlargement, bladder prolapse, and pelvic musculature problems) associated with aging, or may be the result of other medical disorders, such as infections and diabetes mellitus. Because there are a number of treatable conditions responsible for acute urinary incontinence, a complete medical evaluation should be undertaken, and the patient should not be assumed to be incontinent solely because of dementia. Demented people can have other intercurrent medical problems, and this an area where they are common. A history of the problem and associated medical issues should be obtained from the patient and a relative and a physcial examination performed. Urinalysis, urine culture, and tests for urinary retention and incomplete emptying of the bladder should be done. If a reversible cause is found, vigorous treatment should be instituted.

Urinary incontinence secondary to dementia may be related to changes in the sensory awareness of a full bladder because of neuronal deterioration or due to lack of concentration on the need to void; further, patients may be unable to integrate cognitively the need to void with the need to get to the bathroom. Frequent trips to the bathroom and attending to cues that the patient gives that urination is imminent (touching oneself in pelvic area or using a key word to signal the need to urinate) may be helpful. Having a commode available in the bedroom or living area may avoid episodes caused by not getting to the bathroom fast enough. Disposable absorbent underwear with a large capacity for urine may be necessary. In-dwelling catheters should be avoided because of the risk of infection. There are visiting nursing services in many communities that specialize in dealing with aspects of care of demented people. A consultation with them for incontinence might be helpful.

Fecal incontinence usually occurs late in the course of dementia and is related to neuronal deterioration, lack of awareness, and constipation with overflow. Attention to diet and fluid intake and adequate fiber intake is essential. The effects of dementia, usually decreased exercise, and medications tend to make the patient more vulnerable to bowel problems. Regular morning and evening bathroom stops should be instituted. Enemas, several times per week, may be needed to eliminate intractable constipation if all else fails.

Incontinence can be the last straw for many caregivers; others learn to adapt to the procedures, garments, and techniques that help minimize incontinence and the distress it causes. The emotional condition of the caregiver, the extent to which he or she has assistance and relief, and the condition and prognosis of the patient figure into the decision to maintain the patient at home in the face of the development of any major new symptom, such as incontinence. Families who want to continue to care for the patient at home may need increased assistance and professional advice to get over the hurdle of coping.

PSYCHOTIC SYMPTOMS. Some of the psychotic or irrational symptoms have been previously mentioned, particularly as they are the related to memory failure and distortion. Hallucinations are abnormal sensory experiences in which a person sees, hears, smells, feels, or tastes something that is in fact not present. Hallucinations may occur in severe depressions, schizophrenia, a number of organic brain disorders, and as adverse effects of some medications. They may occur in the middle to late stage of dementia, but when they occur, it is important to ensure that they are not the result of other causes. One patient with dementia heard a repetitive song in her head, and another was sure that she saw someone coming into the house through the window at night. No amount of disagreement and heated discussion with the woman would convince her that she did not have unwanted guests. Delusions (false, fixed beliefs) may occur in a variety of disorders, including dementia. Paranoid delusions are the most common type and usually involve someone stealing money or things or someone doing something potentially hurtful to the patient.

Hallucinations and delusions cannot be argued away by the caregiver or anyone else. Neither should they be confirmed. Instead, the caregiver or relative should say that he or she does not see or hear anything or know about the stealing (or any other similar problem), but it sounds frightening and perhaps the patient would like some company. Neuroleptic (tranquilizing, antipsychotic) medications usually reduce the symptoms and should be used if the hallucinations and delusions seriously interfere with functioning or care. Because the patient sees nothing "wrong" with them, the caregiver and family have to present the idea of medication as helpful in reducing the worry or fear associated with these phenomena.

AMNESIA AND APHASIA. Amnesia, or memory loss, and aphasia, an inability to speak, are two of the hallmark clinical symptoms of dementia, particularly Alzheimer's disease. The memory disturbances are usually the first symptoms of dementia, and they are also responsible for many of the secondary behavior problems that occur as the disease progresses and the memory fails. Forgetting facts, events, names, orientation cues, how to perform a task, and the location of objects, money, and other valuables results in frustration and anger. Lost or misplaced items can serve as the focus of delusions about "someone" stealing or hiding things that are important. Patients may forget that a visit or telephone call from a relative or friend occurred and then feel angry or sad that they are being neglected. Or the patient may forget a conversation that just occurred and repetitively telephone someone with whom he or she just spoke. The degree of the amnesia determines the extent to which patients can still take charge of aspects of their own care, including the reliable dispensing of medications. As the disease progresses, the patient will forget the names of close relatives, including the spouse's and even his or her own. These patients may respond to verbal reminders, labeled photographs, and signs bearing the useful words. They may accuse the spouse or other close relatives of being strangers, of intruding in the house, or even of intending to do harm. These are all the product of the brain damage, and although greatly distressing, particularly to the spouse or other caregiver who may have devoted months, even years, of care, they are not reflections of the patient's ingratitude but rather of the extent of the disease.

Aphasia, which begins as a word-finding problem, may progress to the use of words incorrectly, the use of words that sound like the wanted word, or a description of the object or activity rather than the actual word (e.g., "to tell time" = *clock*). The caregiver's guessing at and supplying the correct or sought-after word is sometimes relieving to the patient at the earlier stages, although later the patient will not recognize it. The decreased use of words and eventually a nonverbal state occur in the middle to late stages of the disorder. Similarly, the patient will have diminished ability to understand concepts and words expressed by others, and caregivers will need to modify communication techniques when this occurs. The gradual decrease in a patient's ability to communicate is distressing and frustrating to the patient and to the caregiver. It makes care of the patient more difficult because the patient cannot state wants and needs and marks a significant change in the quality of the relatedness between the patient and other people, particularly close family. Although facial expressions and other nonverbal cues can communicate feelings, the loss of language and the associated disabilities usually signify the end of the companionable relationship that previously existed between the patient and spouse or other relatives. This brings a period of increased stress and loss for all concerned.

Alzheimer's disease is a progressively deteriorative illness, a form of dementia, that ultimately results in brain failure. Its cause is unknown, although dysfunctions of neurotransmitters and receptors in the brain probably play an important role in its etiology. It is possible that Alzheimer's disease is actually a clinical description of several disorders, about which we will learn more as diagnostic tools become more sophisticated. Patients decline slowly, over seven to ten years, with a global loss of intellectual functioning and psychiatric and neurological disability. There is no known definitive treatment, but care directed at maintaining function and treating target symptoms is useful. Demented patients benefit from the active treatment of complicating factors, such as depression, and medical disorders, such as painful arthritis, that add to their emotional stress. Caregivers take on an enormous task and must be attentive not only to the patient's welfare but to their own. In addition to a supportive, caring physician who may offer guidance and medical assistance during the course of the illness, support groups such as those offered by local chapters of the Alzheimer's Association are invaluable to the caregiver, family members, and the patient.

There is much research directed at finding improved diagnostic techniques and various treatment modalities. Research protocols at university medical centers and other institutions to test the effectiveness of new medications and behavioral treatments for dementia may incidentally benefit the patient and caregiver.

They receive a period of intensive assessment, care, and support in the process of such studies, and the effort may give them some hope that they are contributing to the discovery of an eventual cure. That search, in the next decade or two, will result in our ability to make early, more exact diagnoses, offer solutions to the puzzle of causation, and suggest treatments that are definitive and curative.

11

In Conclusion: Being Older and Wiser

Children yearn to be big, to be adults. They think that adults do not have homework, can stay up late at night, and do whatever they want. Adolescents attempt to discover themselves and to deal with their emerging identities, their awkward bodies, and their rising hormones more successfully. We look back on adolescence and are glad we made it past that period. Young adults struggle to define themselves with relationships, education, work, and status. In midlife we deal with the joys and stresses of deepening relationships, family, jobs, and careers; this can be a time of great fulfillment and some frustration. In the later years, we have new concerns of uncertainty, vulnerability, losses, health, death, and others, but we also have the ability to take stock, to reconcile our past and use it wisely to cope and enjoy the present and future. All of this development concerns growing, hopefully, older and wiser.

We are never full grown. Development and growth are continuous through various stages, over a lifetime. There may be fits and starts, plateaus and leaps, but it goes on for most people. Since we all know many 80- and 90-year-olds, who, like Erik Erikson, have demonstrated the process of continued growth by using their talents, choices, and good fortune, we know it is possible, and not necessarily rare. Unfortunately, many people see the later years as a retirement from life, and they do as much as possible to stunt their growth because they think "that's what it is to be old." In the coming years, more and more people will be old, and more of them will demonstrate their abilities to grow.

The older population in the United States is increasing rapidly, from 13 percent of the total population in 1992, including over 32 million people over the age of 65, to more than double that in the year 2030. We are living longer and the group of long-livers, over 85 years of age, is the fastest-growing segment of the population. At age 65, having already survived many of the diseases and accidents that kill younger people, women have an average life expectancy of almost another twenty years, and men can live, on average, for at least another fifteen. Sixty-five is not old by almost anyone's standards other than a 20-year-old's, and an additional fifteen or twenty years is a long time to waste in retirement from life. There is enough time to start new careers, learn new skills, develop new interests, and enjoy new hobbies. In the coming years, because there will be more people over the ages of 65, 75, and 85 than ever before, there will be new strategies and programs for dealing with the problems of later life and for enjoying the perogatives of that era. The elderly will be an increasingly large constituency from which policymakers will hear and to which they will have to answer.

There is no doubt that growing older brings with it trials and troubles, but there is equally no doubt that if we focus on those aspects of life, we may have little else for which to live. One man in his 70s put it this way: "It's somewhat like having a good old automobile. You've gotten used to it; it's fairly reliable, and you know its pluses and minuses. It needs regular maintenance, and, sooner or later, some parts are going to wear out and break down. You fix it and keep it going because it's too expensive to buy a new one. Even though the body's not as good as new, you get a real kick out of washing and shining it up. It's been with you for a long time; you should take care of it."

Our bodies and minds are at least as important to take care of as our metaphorical automobiles. Attention to a nutritious diet, exercise, interesting and enjoyable activities, and socializing with friends, neighbors, and/or family members should be vigorous and constant. These are elements of prevention of physical and mental deterioration. Regular visits to a competent physician who understands the body and mind of an older person prevent some medical problems, while ensuring treatment of those disorders that are already apparent.

Being older and wiser means taking stock of oneself, using the attributes, skills, and knowledge accumulated over a lifetime, and living one's life to the fullest extent possible in chosen ways. It means giving up stereotypes of what older people are supposed to be and looking more to what one can be and do. It means valuing and using lifelines of relationships, experiences, and inherent capabilities—a lifelong storehouse of assets, of which most people never take advantage. Being older and wiser means trying to relate to siblings, children, grandchildren, and friends with mutual concern, support, and love, because there is much to be lost on all sides otherwise. It means treating the disabilities and illnesses that occur seriously, as we would with that valued old car, so that we maximize our function in as many ways as possible. It means trying to heal from the pain of losses that seem excruciating, while knowing that some scars will always remain. It means having to confront our own mortality. It means having the memories of good and bad times in which we have grown, learned, and laughed. It means not getting bogged down in the inevitable aches and pains but, rather, looking for ways to cope so that they can be bypassed, even temporarily.

Being older and wiser means planning for the future, though the future is uncertain and sometimes bleak. It means actively making choices that are in our interest and for those who are important to us. Being older and wiser is living life, whether that means playing cards, fishing, taking care of family and friends, working hard on a job, learning new things, or relaxing on the front porch, to savor what is good and cope with what is not, and hundreds of other things. Being older and wiser means trying to do as much as we want of maybe all of these and continuing to grow in all kinds of ways.

Recommended Additional Reading

American Psychiatric Association. *Diagnostic and Statistical Manual of Mental Disorders*. 3d ed., rev. Washington, D.C.: American Psychiatric Association, 1987.

Belsky, Janet K. *Here Tomorrow*. Baltimore: Johns Hopkins University Press, 1988.

Billig, Nathan. *To Be Old and Sad: Understanding Depression in the Elderly*. Lexington, MA, Lexington Books (Macmillan), 1987.

Butler, Robert N. *Why Survive? Being Old in America*. New York: Harper & Row, 1975.

Carlin, Vivian F., and Mansberg, Ruth. *Where Can Mom Live?* Lexington, MA, Lexington Books, 1987.

Erikson, Erik H. *Childhood and Society*. New York: Norton, 1963.

———. *The Life Cycle Completed*. New York: Norton, 1982.

———, Erikson, J. M., and Kivnik, H. Q. *Vital Involvement in Old Age*. New York: Norton, 1986.

Green, Stephen. *Mind and Body*. Washington, D.C.: American Psychiatric Press, 1985.

Jarvik, Lissy, and Small, Gary. *Parentcare*. New York: Crown, 1988.

Mace, Nancy L., and Rabins, Peter V. *The 36-Hour Day*. Baltimore: Johns Hopkins University Press, 1991.

Meshinsky, Joanne. *How to Choose a Nursing Home*. New York: Avon Books, 1991.

Moak, G. S., Stein, E. M., and Rubin, J. E. V. *The Over-50 Guide to Psychiatric Medications*. Washington, D.C.: American Psychiatric Association, 1989.

Roth, Phillip. *Patrimony*. New York: A Touchstone Book, 1991.

Viorst, Judith. *Necessary Losses*. New York: Simon and Schuster, 1986.

Walz, Thomas H., and Blum, Nancee S. *Sexual Health in Later Life*. Lexington, MA, Lexington Books, 1987.

Index